LIFE STRUGGLES:

AN AUTOBIOGRAPHIC RECORD OF

THE EARLIER TRIALS AND LATER TRIUMPHS

OF THE

REV. JAMES INCHES HILLOCKS,

Author of "Mission Life in London;" "Christian Revivals;" &c., and General
Superintendent of The Christian Union for Christian Work.

EDITED, WITH REMARKS,

BY THE REV. GEORGE GILFILLAN, M.A.,

Author of "The Bards of the Bible," &c.

The larger portion of this Volume is based on Mr Hillocks' "Life Story."

GLASGOW:
JOHN S. MARR & SONS, 194 BUCHANAN STREET.
LONDON: SIMPKIN, MARSHALL AND CO.
1876.

"His motto through his severe Life Struggle has been the very brief but most pregnant sentence—I'll rise again!—expressing in one terse phrase his energy as a Man, and his hope as a Christian."

CONTENTS.

	PAGE
DEDICATION,	5
EDITOR'S PREFACE,	9

CHAPTER I.
First Struggles to Live, ... 13

CHAPTER II.
Earlier Struggles to Learn, ... 19

CHAPTER III.
The Combat Deepens, ... 27

CHAPTER IV.
On the Tramp, ... 36

CHAPTER V.
Thrice Saved on One Sunday, ... 43

CHAPTER VI.
Things Working Together for Good, ... 48

CHAPTER VII.
The Dawn Darkened, ... 55

CHAPTER VIII.
The Teacher in his First School, ... 67

CHAPTER IX.
Other Schools and Other Scholars, ... 77

CONTENTS.

CHAPTER X.
Sudden Changes, ... 87

CHAPTER XI.
From Dundee and Back, ... 98

CHAPTER XII.
In Edinburgh Once More, ... 109

CHAPTER XIII.
At Work in the Garret, ... 116

CHAPTER XIV.
The Last of his Scottish Struggles, ... 123

CHAPTER XV.
A Tribute—Departed Friends, ... 129

CHAPTER XVI.
More Stepping-Stones to London, ... 139

CHAPTER XVII.
Thoughts on Leaving for London, ... 147

CHAPTER XVIII.
The *Resumé*—From December, 1860, ... 156

CHAPTER XIX.
The *Resumé* Continued, ... 170

DEDICATION.

TO JAMES COX, Esq., Ex-Provost of Dundee.

My Dear Friend,

My little book, "Life Story: a Prize Autobiography," was dedicated to Maggie, my beloved helpmeet. This I did as a mark of sincere gratitude to God, for the aid she so lovingly and bravely rendered in the midst of our struggles for life and usefulness, "with all the fortitude of a true woman's moral heroism."

And the dedication of this volume—"Life Struggles."—to you calls forth additional thoughts of gratitude, many of which are associated with the early days of preparation, in what was then the small village of Lochee—in which the name you bear has had, and still has, a remarkable and beneficial influence. There I was the "Young Weaver" employed by you; then, too, it was that you and your worthy brothers kindly encouraged the young lad to persevere in his onward course; and this, let me add, was done in a spirit that is still characteristic of the large firm of the enterprising members of which you are the oldest.

But pleasing as it is thus to remember that "kind words can never die," the thought is greatly enhanced by the fact that he whose sympathetic words soothed and animated, has himself perseveringly triumphed, rising in social position and Christian usefulness—becoming the Chief Magistrate of my native town—one of the leading commercial centres of this great nation.

I say "Christian usefulness," and rejoice that this can be added; for, after all, to me this is the chief source of attraction—that in which we are of one mind and one heart.

Such, Dear Friend, is an indication of the reasons why I desire that your name and influence go with this volume; and hence I rejoice that you have so readily and kindly complied with my wish.

I have referred to "Life Story," because it forms the basis of the larger portion of this work; and I may state, in passing, that the latest edition of that autobiography was 5000 copies. It has been out of print for some time, while the calls for copies have been increasing, especially since the Railway Collision at Harrow, in which I nearly lost my life.

The labour of editing "Life Struggles" has been generously undertaken by my warm and constant friend, the Rev. George Gilfillan. As you know, this is only one of the many proofs of his hearty desire to help those who are endeavouring to rise. He has done more than linked the passages together. As you will find, his occasional remarks are to the point, and are likely to be useful. You will, I am sure, agree with me in my conviction, that I have reason to be thankful because of this proof of his hearty kindness.

This letter, I fear, is already sufficiently long, and yet I would hope that another sentence or two may not be out of place here. Whatever strength or charm the Editor may add to the work, it *is* an "Autobiography," and in this *I* am deeply concerned. Almost every one who writes an autobiography presents an apology for doing so. But why? If it is *proper* to give a record of some of the several features of one's own life, then no apology is necessary. If it is *wrong* to do so, an apology cannot mend the matter. Perhaps it is the severe pouncing upon the pronoun "I" that frightens such writers; but every thoughtful reader knows that an autobiography is necessarily subjective, and must involve the frequent use of that pronoun. Knowing this, and knowing that apologies are awkward offerings, and seldom accepted, I shall rather give a brief word of explanation.

It has been said that an autobiography cannot be "excused" unless there is something extraordinary in the narrative, or unless the writer has reached the crowning-point of a brilliant career, having worked his way to a position at once lofty and distinct. Now "lofty," as a qualifying term, is calculated to frighten one who does not belong to the tall class, especially if he is conscious of having lived a humble life. And this is my weak point. The truth is, I am still pressing onward, though, I trust, rising upward. Indeed, my position in the great "Life Drama" has never been very exalted, socially at least. Looking from that point, my life has been what some would call commonplace, and may be regarded as the life of almost all who have lived among the lowly; but who, by God's help, *have tried to raise themselves and those around them*. And hence I lay no claim to any special mark of distinction separating me from those who have struggled as I have struggled, and laboured as I have laboured, to be useful. It would be sheer hypocrisy on my part to say I have neither special ability nor large experience in relation to the life I have endeavoured to lead. That would be a species of sham humility which honesty detests. God in His providence and by His grace has trained me (severely, I sometimes thought) for my mission, and I have endeavoured, in the Name and Spirit of my Saviour, to sustain the responsibilities connected with whatever work He has given me—whether as Teacher, Evangelist, or Pastor. Yet it would be as unbecoming in me as it is distant from my desire to think of setting myself above my fellow-labourers—those earnest hard workers who have perseveringly striven to help the weak and raise the fallen.

But though my position alone cannot "excuse" the publication of this narrative—*if we are bound by the rule just given*—yet I may be pardoned when it is remembered that I was urged to write the autobiography; that it gained a *first* prize; that the late Professor Nichol was one of the adjudicators; and that the three specified conditions which gave the MSS. a place in the competition were these—"That the lives be genuine narratives, that they be told with a fair share of intelligence and perspicuity, and that they possess breadth of representative character and fitness to afford practical suggestion and encouragement."

If this was in any degree realized in the smaller volume, surely the chances are greater under the kindly care of the able Editor.

    I am, Dear Friend,
        Yours most respectfully in all good work,
            J. I. HILLOCKS.

Eden House,
   127 Stoke Newington Road, London, November, 1876.

EDITOR'S PREFACE.

How uninteresting is the course of a canal, with its sluggish uniformity; or of a lazy low country river, like the Cam—"the sleeping river," as Hall calls it, "standing still to see people drown themselves." How different from a Highland torrent, resisted at every step by some rocky obstacle against which it boldly rushes and fiercely or gaily overcomes—here fretted into the picturesque, there lashed into the sublime, and yonder tormented into the terribly beautiful—its power developed by contradiction, and its passion provoked by controversy.

So it is in life. All men worthy of the name, are so indebted to, and identified with, struggle, that it has become difficult to conceive of virtue or excellence without it. And many have conceived its extent, in a modified form, to a future world; and have fancied that the "River of Life" hereafter may be grander and more divine, too, if shaded by forests, flung over cataracts, and contesting its immortal way with crags and precipices, than flowing smoothly through gardens of everlasting bloom.

But be that as it may, this we know, struggle is the wise law of humanity; and, as such, should be welcomed, not only with submission, but also with joy. Sometimes it may be that struggle sours and exasperates; but let it not be forgotten, that those upon whom it produces bad effects would possibly have been worse under a different training. At all events, it is a pleasing thought that so many pilgrims of progress are climbing the hill of Difficulty, that so many heroes are pantingly following the banner on which Excelsior is inscribed. And, as we shall see, among those who have thus struggled upward is our friend Mr Hillocks, whose remarkable career on this and the other side of the Border we have watched with unflagging interest. In his heroic efforts—no less for usefulness than for life—we see a correct translation of Longfellow's Latin into the manly vernacular of Burns—

> "Man's a sodger,
> And life's but a faught."

To his case, in the stern preparation for the special work on which he has long ago so heartily entered, among the seething masses of London, we may apply the line of Dr Johnson, which was printed in capitals—

> "Slow rises worth by poverty depressed."

But to us, and doubtless to the reader, the manner in which such men, through incredible suffering and hard toil, work their own way to the desired haven, of even comparative success, is very interesting. Hence it is with no common pleasure that we set ourselves to the task of connecting some of the more instructive passages from the revised and enlarged copy of his "Story," offering such occasional remarks as the incidents may suggest.

Thus amply furnished with matter in type and in MS., we have had no difficulty in our endeavour to sustain the idea clearly indicated by the second part of the title—"An Autobiographic Record"—but we have thought it proper to omit many of his more lengthy remarks on social, educational, and religious topics, even when given in connection with some of the passages in his life. With the view of avoiding the risk of encumbering the narrative, we have suggested that at a suitable time his more important reflections on the questions of the day may be published in a separate form, to which the reader could turn as time permitted and inclination directed. Certainly his experience gives weight to his observations.

It should also be stated that the MS. provided had in it some interesting matter from other pens than his own. For instance, here is what one of his "literary associates" very properly calls a "characteristic anecdote."

This friend, who has also risen, tells us what we have elsewhere noticed, that "Mr Hillocks belonged to one of the best of those Literary Societies for which Dundee has been renowned, and which has done so much to sharpen the brightest intellects and form the finest tastes of that busy city. On one occasion he had incurred the displeasure of the Chairman, who delivered a fierce Philippic as a punishment. This the young lad regarded as unfair, and made several attempts to show that the statements to which he had listened were *ex parte*. These efforts so roused the Chairman that he lost both patience and temper—imperatively exclaiming, 'Sit down, Sir! I say, sit down.'

" 'I'll sit down,' said Mr Hillocks, suiting the action to the word; 'but I'll *rise* again.'

"This he did, and soon conquered by sheer persistence. And here we have the key-note to all that follows—the effort and success which, under God's blessing, led, and is still leading, to increasing usefulness. The incident is slight in itself, but it most aptly illustrates the character of the man—that indomitable perseverance which has ever been one of his leading characteristics, and which has not been weakened by misfortune, nor crushed down by opposition. His motto through his severe life-struggles, has been the very brief, but most pregnant, sentence—'I'll rise again!'—expressing in one terse phrase, his energy as a man, and his hope as a Christian."

This is the key-note to what follows. Mr Hillocks has often been cast down, but only to rise again, and generally higher than before. And this, we submit, is the stuff which forms the backbone of all our most useful biographies.

LIFE STRUGGLES.

CHAPTER I.

FIRST STRUGGLES TO LIVE.

HIS BIRTHPLACE.

THOSE who have listened to Mr Hillocks' lecture on "Scotland and the Scotch," have learned that he is a Scotchman, and that he loves his native land. He was born in Dundee.

This busy town has now become a fashionable centre in the north; but there were in it some queer primitive places, with ancient manners, such, for instance, as in the Blackscroft, which may be called our Alsatia, only without its special wickedness, where a flight of stairs conducts you from the main street into the centre of the eighteenth century—so much did the thatched cottages and homely antique habitues of the people differ from those of their neighbours. Another of these spots—which at the time of his birth was a quiet region—is the Bonnethill. It is separated from the bustling quarters of the town by a long and very steep brae, after climbing which, if fat and pursy, like Hamlet,

"With labour dire, and weary woe,"

you found yourself in a very peculiar locality, tenanted chiefly by handloom weavers, a race that has all but disappeared.

It was in one of such tenements where the humble parents of our friend lived and laboured, and where he was born on the morning of the 7th of April, but we are not certain as to the exact year.

Speaking of that event, he says, "Of astrology, I know nothing save that it is defined as the pretended science of foretelling the fate of man by the star under which he is born, or the month in which he saw the light. But I have often thought that April was a somewhat fitting symbol of what followed. As everybody knows, April is noted for being fickle. During its stay with us, we may have a lovely and sunshiny day, but the very next one may be rough and rainy, with blasts almost wintry. Now, we may have a delightful view—the smiling sunbeams dancing on the bright green of the fresh leaves and the opening flowers; then, of a sudden, the whole of this beauty is obscured by dark and frowning clouds. Now an agreeable warmth, as on a beautiful summer morning; then an unpleasant chill as on a wet winter night.

"If I have not had all the sunshine of an April, I have had very many of its chilling blasts, and these at the very commencement of my life."

HIS PARENTAGE.

To his parentage, Mr Hillocks thus pays an affectionate tribute. "I leave," he says, "the tracing of pedigrees to those who plume themselves on the title, the rank, or the wealth of their ancestry. With me,

> 'The pith o' sense, the pride o' worth
> Are higher far than a' that.'

I may, however, remark that my parents belonged to the real working classes—those who cheerfully work for their bread, and live to be useful.

"Of my mother, I can only speak from hearsay, but her love and purity are the more valuable to me that I have not known their decay. To this day they are as unsullied as when first I heard of them from the lips of those who had known her from infancy till she departed for Paradise.

"My father, too, was worthy of my mother, and that is saying much, not too much. When a mere boy he became an apprentice sailor, and was afterwards 'pressed' into 'His Majesty's Service.' At 'the peace,' in 1815, he was 'paid off'—the best of his days—his robust health and remarkable strength—having passed away while with others rendering our grim bulwarks terrible. I may be wrong, yet I have often thought that he was shamefully treated, considering what he did for the nation. Ever since I was able to reflect, it has stung me to the heart to think that a man so noble and brave should have been so cruelly neglected. He, however, like all real men, made the best of his fate.

"After ploughing the deep for full fifteen years, he, on returning home, betook himself to the loom as a means of living. Even yet, I think I see him at that weary loom, brave as ever, the peculiar clink of the rapid shuttle keeping time to the simple notes of a sea-ditty. When he was not so racked by pain, as he often was—when poverty had not appeared in the more hideous forms which it often assumed—he was cheerful. It was truly touching to see him during these brief intervals from dire distress, and to hear him, while weaving, singing with considerable emotion—

'All in the Downs our fleet lay moored.'

Though he suffered long, he retained the heroic spirit of the real British Tar to the last—deeply imbued with a love of right and truth. He was a patriot in the true sense of the term. It was the impulse of a genuine patriotism that gave energy to him as one of the thousands of those guards, who so nobly defended our little 'Isle of the sea;' and though he was left to suffer the pains and penalties of honest poverty, he did not forget to instil into our young minds that heart-felt love of country which inspires the soul, leads to the defence of truth, the gaining of right, and the maintaining of freedom."

HIS FIRST MISFORTUNE.

With considerable force and feeling, he thus refers to what he calls his first misfortune,—the loss of his mother. "I am told that for a few days matters went on favourably, and my parents were led to rejoice and to foster their fondest hopes. But soon their joys gave way to sorrow, for shortly mournful wailings took the place of the bright prospects. My mother became seriously ill, and died on the twenty-first day after I was born."

Who can tell the amount of sadness contained in the latter part of that brief statement? To the busy world around, this was but a casual event, yet its effects were severely felt by all concerned, especially this motherless child. The loss of a mother in youth becomes a most important circumstance in the history of the life of struggle. The loss of the father is truly painful, but the fatherless may be strengthened by that energy, which Forster describes as desertion ministering to the manly and courageous, like the ivy which he saw, when the support of the oak was withdrawn, asserted its independence, and shot out into a bold elastic stem. A father dies, and the protection of his roof is withdrawn; but that might have been a shelter to indolence. The fatherless boy is compelled to go out into the world, and as all retreat is cut off behind him, he is thrown on his own resources, and his powers, as if inspired by the spirit of his departed sire, develop rapidly into maturity, and his energies enable him to surmount difficulty and attain heights at which he himself is astonished. But the death of a mother takes away an important shield in the battle of life, and the motherless combatant, if weak, may at times be defeated. At all events, the ills of life are likely to fall fast around him—as our friend soon found.

As a matter of course, he was put under a wet nurse. But she treated him very cruelly for nearly two years. Speaking from what he had afterwards heard from those who knew him in his infancy, he says,—" Her wilful neglect and rash drugging made me a weaker child than I was when my mother died. This paved the way for numerous diseases, which followed each other in rapid succession, weakening my constitution, and stunting my growth."

PRESSED INTO SERVICE.

At the end of these two years of bad treatment, the lad and his sister were taken home to their stepmother—the sailor-weaver having married again. And, under the new regime, he made such progress that when about three years of age he began to walk. But soon after this, and long before he was at all able, the poor child was pressed into service, becoming a winder even before he could reach the spokes of the wheel, the feet of which had to be cut shorter that he might be able to drive it. Here he sat working hard, the wonder of many a visitor, he being so young and so little. Not much sleep, nor much food, and less pure air; no play to cheer him, nor healthy out-door exercise to strengthen his weak limbs, he suffered much. Well might he afterwards exclaim—" Who can know a tenth of the heart-breaking sufferings which must be endured by the sons and daughters of the poor?" To this important question, he replies—" None save those who have been so unfortunate as to know them by sad experience. Their misery is great even when their parents are guided by worldly prudence, supported by fortitude, and cheered by

Christian hope. Hard, hard is the heart that would not weep for the sorrows of the poor man's children; and cruel, cruel is the system which keeps them in poverty, hunger, and dirt." "Generally," he adds, "I had to drive the wheel from four in the morning till ten at night, the long day which my poor father had to weave to support his family. No wonder then I have not become a giant in stature.

CHAPTER II.

EARLIER STRUGGLES TO LEARN.

THE AWAKENING OF THE DESIRE TO LEARN.

It has been said that few can read Mr Hillocks' "Life Story" without tears and smiles. There is "an air of child-like simplicity" about the "Story," but there is also a quiet humour which frequently comes out, often side by side with touching pathos. Of this we have an instance in the chapter we are about to give.

Notwithstanding what we have read, he brightens up, and tells us, that "Hope looked *in*, and said, 'Look *up!*'" and then adds, "Dark as the clouds were, there was a silver lining occasionally."

To the poor, a little seems much, if it comes when most wanted. It was so in the case of our young hero. A tiny ray lit up his naturally happy face from time to time. And the first we hear of comes in the form of "a little leisure at meal times." The next took the shape of the additional favour of a run out in the *gloamins* with other boys and girls, both of which benefits were to him a source of great pleasure. But these breathing times were destined to give more than mere recreation. By means of this favour he formed the acquaintance of more fortunate children, who went to school, and who could read and write. The knowledge of this, and his conversations with them, soon created in him the wish to be able to do likewise. And this desire so greatly increased, that, of his own accord, he lessened his play-time; so much so that whenever he had the opportunity he was seen among those four or five times his age, listening to others reading or discussing.

This desire to learn was strengthened by a domestic incident which we record in his own words. "One morning," he says, "the family were all concerned in the reading of a letter from America, where some of my stepmother's relatives had gone to push their fortune. Those relatives said they loved me; they also promised to send for me *when I was big*. The Americans seem to like big people and big things; and perhaps that accounted for the saving clause which gave me not a little trouble. At last, I became as uncharitable as to suppose they knew I never would be "big"—at least, they never sent for me. Yet the incident was not lost on me; for though I did not get to America, I got to school."

Seeing he could not reach the better feelings of those abroad, he applied all the eloquence he could command at home, until his desire was somewhat gratified. He says, "At last my father consented, notwithstanding the many difficulties which stood in the way—difficulties the power of which none but the poor weaver and a suffering family can know. That was to me an important day, on which I received my A B C card and the twopenny fee! With the heart light as the lark at rising day, I left home that morning; and for three months I continued to work in the morning, go to school at ten, and work in the evening. I was often very tired, but I was glad. Soon I became the teacher's pet. He would pat me on the head and say, I would soon become the best scholar in his school. And then he had such a gem of a wife, who loved me as if I had been her own child—a mild woman, full of calm dignity and common sense. We all loved her, and I am glad I was able to do her the last favour she needed on earth."

This "joyous prosperity" reached the climax at the end of the third month. He says, "The master added to my joy when he pronounced me ready for the Bible and Collection. I soon transmitted this news to my parents; but imagine my disappointment and grief when I was told there was no money to purchase the books, and that I must leave school, and give all my time to the *pirn* wheel! But grief was somewhat modified by my father assuring me he was glad to find that his effort to give me a few weeks at the school was not fruitless. I should have been thankful, and perhaps I was, but I was sorrowful too. Of this I am sure, I was anxious to retain what I had received of the ability to read. This was done by the purchasing of little story-books with the halfpence I had given me by those who came to see me at the wheel. It was my delight to follow out the 'magic paths of the nursery tales.' No miser could hunt for gold with deeper interest than I tried to trace what to me were the absorbing incidents of 'Jack, the Giant Killer,' 'Cock Robin,' the 'Babes in the Wood,' and all the other little books I could obtain."

THE "YOUNG WEAVER'S" STUDY.

In the course of time our young friend was raised from the "weary wheel" to the dubious elevation of the "sickening loom." Here at the very outset of his "ascent in the labour scale," an almost insurmountable difficulty presented itself, but even as early as this, he proved the truth of one of his favourite phrases—that "difficulties are not impossibilities." He was so young and so little that he could not, without assistance, either reach the cloth and yarn beams or trample the treddles; but by the aid of an ingenious erection and heavy clogs he was able to proceed.

It does not seem that this "elevation," from the wheel to the loom, added to his physical comfort; but it enabled him to help the family, and that was a gratification of no ordinary nature. Because of the sad state of his father's health, the family—especially at this severe time, and after—were often reduced to the direst poverty. Referring to one of those "terrible times," our young friend says, "So severe were our sufferings, that I have known three weeks pass without a penny coming in save what I worked for. How could this keep life in a whole family? During such times of hard pressure I have worked twenty-four hours on ends—and that on a few table-spoonfuls of pease-meal made into what we called *brose*. Often have I heard my father groaning with pain while the poor children were crying in vain for food."

And yet he, almost in the same breath, assures us, that "It was not *all* darkness;" that a ray of hope forced its way into this home, imparting a little grateful joy. His desire to learn was inextinguishable. Amid excessive toil and the severe pangs of starvation, he thought of self-culture and applied whatever likely means were within his reach. He had somewhere met with this couplet—

> "Despair of nothing, good you would attain;
> Unwearied diligence your point will gain."

These words would come to him again and again, especially when greatly depressed and almost overcome, strengthening him for the unequal fight against all but overwhelming circumstances. Whenever there was the least opportunity—when the high pressure of cutting want would permit—he devoted to reading his few spare moments, and gradually became more and more interested in learning the elements of what is called school education.

His description of his "first study" which he at this time occupied, is somewhat picturesque. He says, "Had you entered the village of Lochee, near Dundee, and gone along the South-road, till you came to a long row of low-roofed thatched houses, and entered the second door from the west, you would have seen a four-loomed shop in the one end, and a kitchen in the other. This was my abode. Had you looked in at the kitchen door, you would have seen towards your right the form of a curtain bed and two chairs, not so good as they had been. Close to the wall, opposite to the bed, was a roughly-finished dresser over which was placed an old plate-rack, and on which were some crockery. To the right there was what was called the *timmer bedstead*, the lids of which were constantly kept close to keep out the tow dust which was flying everywhere. Beside this unhealthy bed was a chest of drawers minus the better-half of the handles, and on the top were a variety of school-books, the 'Life of Dr Franklin,' 'Self-culture,' other small works of a similar nature, and a number of the Anti-Bread Tax Society's Tracts, and the Chartist Circular. These made up my library.

"Had you entered this sham of a house, this ill-ventilated hovel, between the long and short hours of twelve and one, when all, nine in number, were asleep save myself, you would have found me standing in front the said chest of drawers, sometimes writing, sometimes casting-up figures, and sometimes reading and taking a peep at history.

"This was my 'study.' It can neither be commended for its elegance nor its comfort, yet there are associations connected with it that impart a kind of sweet melancholy which I cannot describe. In one sense, it was not a bad college in which to be trained." This same house, but now considerably improved, is called "Hillocks' College" to this day.

HIS "JUVENILE WAILINGS."

So he soon took to the midnight oil. Nor was he less active in the daytime, taxing himself with a given portion of work from early morning. When that portion was finished before the hour was up, he would rest and read till the time expired. These moments, he adds, "I devoted to the reading of the speeches and lectures of the great agitators of the day—a species of reading in which I took a great delight, and from which I derived much profit."

But, as might have been expected, the health of our weaver-student broke down under this truly hard and active life. It brought on a dangerous attack of inflammation which laid him aside for a time, yet he no sooner recovered than he started again as cheerful and as hopeful as ever. We should say, as hopeful and cheerful as the circumstances would permit; for it is evident that he has been subject to those strong emotions which bespeak a sensitive nature as well as an aspiring soul. And this has been from early youth, as appears in one of his "Juvenile Wailings." Speaking of the occasion which wrung from his heart the following verses, he says, "Then I was about half-way in my teens, as we say in Scotland. I felt very sad and wept bitterly, being cold and hungry, almost to fainting. But I sought a quiet nook wherein to pour out my grief in tears and rhyme; and afterwards called the lines 'My Mammy's Awa'":—

'Cauld, cauld is the day, the frost nips my wee face;
I'm heartless and sad, how waefu' my case!
On my bare wee leggies the bitin' winds blaw—
Oh! hoo is a' this? My Mammy's awa'!

'Baith laddies an' lassies are happy an' gay,
They rin to the schule and then to their play;
But I maun rin errants 'mang frost, sleet, an' snaw—
Oh! hoo is a' this? My Mammy's awa'!

'They a' get braw claes, and their head fu' o' lear,
To mak' them a' great, if God should them spare;
But nae schulin' for me, nae learnin' ava'.
Oh! hoo is a' this? My Mammy's awa'!

'Yet onward I'll push, to get lear like the lave,
I'll ever be active, determined, an' brave,
Tho' hard be my fate, it softer may blaw,
For God will prove kind, tho' Mammy's awa'."

He adds, "These lines are all to be found of what was to be published under the title of 'My Juvenile Wailings.' They consisted of forty such pieces, selected from many more, by Mr Campbell, then English Teacher in the Dundee Seminaries, and author of some valuable school-books. But this collection was stolen when ready for the press, and have not been seen since. These four verses, however, had been previously sent to a newspaper, and hence preserved."

We had not the pleasure of seeing these pieces, but Mr Hillocks agreed with Mr Campbell in regarding the theft as a loss; and so it was, if we may judge from his other poems, nearly all of which partake of that *naïveté*, sweet simplicity and child-heartedness which has been properly regarded as one of the leading causes of his success, especially as a teacher.

THE BRIGHT SIXPENCE.

Immediately after this outflow of melting grief and noble resolution, he was seen suiting the action to his words—"Yet onward I'll push to get lear like the lave." And while struggling on against almost overwhelming odds, he perceived the "silver lining of the dark cloud" which had been standing over him for a long time. He says, "My poor dear father became so improved in health, that the family did not depend on my labours as before. And knowing my desire to get the aid of the living voice to tell me if my advances were genuine, he promised to give me sixpence per web—that is, sixpence per week; and this promise he kept as often as possible. This was a useful sixpence. It emitted a tiny ray of hope which greatly and pleasantly warmed and invigorated my heart. Upon this promised sixpence I read the words, 'It is possible.' It enabled me to get to the night-school."

He was very fortunate in his teachers, such as Mr Barrie, the late Messrs Auchterlonie and Doctor, and Rev. George

Hunter. Referring to them and to others, he says—" They had good hearts, and their abilities were of no ordinary nature. They felt interested in their pupils, and were glad to see them advancing."

His advance was rapid, daily becoming more determined to grapple with every obstacle and overcome it if possible. In this resolution he was again aided by his worthy father in a manner which by the son was regarded as generous as well as thoughtful. It was that the latter should pay only his board, and so have more means with which to prosecute his studies. "This offer," he says, "I gladly accepted, and laboured the harder that I might save as much money as would pay a month's board in advance, and thereby get to the school in the daytime also. To my joy, I succeeded. My exertions, means, and knowledge increased. Well do I remember the emotion which lightened my labours, feeling convinced that I was on a fair way to reach the summit of my ambition—the pulpit."

CHAPTER III.

THE COMBAT DEEPENS.

HARD TIMES GROWING HARDER.

HE, by hard work and careful saving, was enabled to go to the day-school, working and learning morning and evening, until, as he says, "Nature, that faithful monitor, seized me as a lawless offender, and stopped my career for a time. Another dangerous illness laid me very low."

Certainly this is not to be wondered at, though it must have been very disappointing to him; apart from the overwork, mental as well as physical, he was surrounded by some of the most disagreeable elements of comfort, in that small low-roofed, damp abode, which he has described, "a very grave." Yet God was there and His blessing. For months the nature of his serious illness became the subject of much talk in the village. The doctor who was first called, finding the complaint baffling his skill, the assistance of a neighbouring physician was procured. Daily, and sometimes thrice a day, they visited and consulted, and still grave doubts were entertained of his recovery. But at last he rallied, and, with that remarkable re-bounding which, in him, has so often manifested itself to the surprise and joy of his friends.

Though it was some considerable time before he recovered so as to be able to work and study as before, yet all was not lost. During his convalescence some books were kindly lent to him, and so closely did he read them that each book left its special stamp on his young mind, which has ever been very impressible, as well as sensitive. As to the impressions then made we shall refer again, simply stating here that this reading to good purpose was not the only result which happily followed this all but fatal illness.

The unexpected recovery led our young hero to pour out his sincere and heartfelt thanks to God, and speak warmly of kind friends, and the kindly care of the medical gentlemen who attended him. This gratitude in the midst of such suffering led one of the gentlemen, Dr Wood, to manifest a continued interest in the weak but undaunted student.

Not knowing what might he the happy result of such special kindness, Dr Wood not only watched the progress of his patient, but gave another turn to his studies—lending him chemical and medical works, and giving him instruction in these valuable sciences. Our friend thus closes a brief record of this special favour.

"Having become the Doctor's pupil, I was often with him till he died. With many more, I lamented his sudden departure in the prime of life. But I am happy to say his teaching was not lost. The lessons he taught led me to wish for further information, and induced me sometime after to resume the study of medicine in relation to disease. And this has been very serviceable to me in my labours among the masses in England as well as Scotland."

But even when all this was making glad the heart of the "Young Weaver," other circumstances were pulling another way, and gradually increased in strength till he was almost overpowered by them. Indeed, as soon as he was at all able to resume work, his leading thoughts and greatest efforts were to pay off whatever debts had been contracted by his father during this illness. And scarcely had he gained this laudable object, and returned to the night-school as before, when labour generally, and weaving particularly, came to "a fearful stand."

He adds, "Most of the work entrusted to the village agents was withdrawn, and wages were soon reduced to the starvation point." At last, it became almost impossible for him to get a web. When any work could be found, the heads of families were first supplied, and his ailing father was seldom able to go so far and wait so long. "The home became once more very empty and very sad."

Nor was his the only home of this kind. In the midst of this general want and terrible misery, the country was agitated from one end to the other; and our young friend, like other young lads, and some in the prime of life, was bit with the Chartist mania. This was not surprising. Hunger, even the hunger of honest poverty, will lead its victims to think strange thoughts and to do startling deeds. In his case, the quiet worker and plodding scholar became what some were pleased to call "the young rebel."

HIS "FIRST INTRODUCTION TO SOCIETY."

This great and unfavourable change was brought about not so much by any special change in his own heart, as by other means. The lad was the same, but the circumstances became more powerful, bringing up with them not a little of the influence of the past. To one ever ready to listen with eagerness, often asking questions, and storing up the answers for after thought, his early training could not but leave its mark, extending even to that phase of politics to which he now felt called upon to look. Without attaching any blame to his father and the friends who sought his company, it is well that parents and guardians see the necessity of being careful lest what they say before children may prove to be too strongly put, even when the thought expressed may not be wrong in itself.

"This want of work," says Mr Hillocks, "and the great

suffering that followed, drew me aside from my main object and led me into society for which, in one sense, I was not prepared, and for which, in another sense, I was somewhat prepared. This was not the first time I was introduced to those holding like views, and it brought to remembrance much that was at that time laid before me."

The time to which he refers is when he was almost a child, "the little *winder*," some said "the little wonder." At that time it was a sight not to be forgotten to see the "Old Tar," with cowl instead of cap or hat, grave and thoughtful face, working patiently at his web, while a copy of a newspaper lay alongside the Bible ready for reference. He was then, and continued to be, a "Radical Reformer," an intelligent member of the "Political Union," one who held to "the Bill, the whole Bill, and nothing but the Bill," until it became law, to the joy and rejoicing of many in Dundee and elsewhere. The boy was taken to the great procession. Sometimes he was led between two men, and sometimes he was carried "shoulder high." From this elevation, he tells us, he saw the hero of the day, George Kinloch of Kinloch, the man whom Dundee yet delights to honour as a politician. The lad was filled with the spirit of the day, and, like others, he shouted "Kinloch for ever!"

In this there was nothing wrong, nor do we find fault with the Radical Reformer instructing his apprentice in politics as well as the art of weaving; but this was not all, there were the warm discussions and the free expressions of strong sentiments of the visitors, and these not only arrested the attention of the young inquirer, but grew still stronger in him until he became more radical than his father.

He gives us an insight of this in a few words on what he humorously calls his "first introduction to society." "The ceremony was neither gorgeous nor gaudy. There was a little vacant curiosity about it, but there was also a hearty generosity

—manifest in half-pence and sometimes a new penny given to me, with which I laid the foundation of my juvenile library. For this, I had to answer many questions on a variety of subjects, domestic and otherwise; but, on the other hand, I was also favoured with an occasional pat on the head and a patronising word of encouragement. My friends and fellow-pupils in the political school were not such as wear gay crosses, bright stars, stiff embroidery, and deal in stiffer manners. By the fashionable it would not be called 'good society,' but certainly it would be wrong to call it 'bad,' in the worst sense of that term. Some would have prefixed to it the word 'vulgar,' because it was not the 'polished politeness' which is often preferred to common sense—that utterance which needs no argument to prove it to be truth. Our reception-room was the four-loom shop, the time was a portion of the meal hour, the subject was the topic of the day, and the result was to make me what my elders called 'the young politician'—a little vain, I fear, of my early training and half knowledge."

If his was half knowledge, the same could not be said of his enthusiasm; the latter was unbounded, notwithstanding the depressing nature of other circumstances. Notwithstanding his father's advice to the contrary, he allowed himself to be led into the midst of the fiery agitation, and became "a public man" while yet a mere boy—he having delivered his first public speech when not more than sixteen years of age. Though he was so agitated during this first attempt that he could scarcely see the crowded, cheering, and hissing audience before him, yet he soon gathered courage and became "ready to meet an antagonist any night."

SOMETHING FOR THE PHILANTHROPIST.

All this seemed to change his nature. The retired boy, with noble aim, entered so heartily into the unhealthy life around him that he really "enjoyed the fun of a stormy meeting," the stormier the nearer to his liking. Nor did he stop here. The young orator also became "Our Own Correspondent" to a newspaper established for the advocacy of the principles he had adopted. In this, too, he put forth his whole energy; and, in the end, became "quite fearless," lashing what he conceived to be wrong, and upholding what he thought was right.

Whether any good came of this outspoken manner we cannot say, but it caused much evil to himself, bringing about much additional personal suffering, amounting at times to persecution. He gives an instance. "Having," he says, "thus spoken and written, those opposed to me sought, in mean and cowardly ways, to punish me; and some, even of the ignoble as well as the cruel, soon proved they had the power as well as the will. And one of the ways was to deprive me of the chance of getting even a share of the work which occasionally found its way to Lochee. For example, one of the manufacturers was fortunate enough to receive an order for work. I had weaved for him before, and he promised me a web as early as possible, and right glad was I even of the promise. But the 'foresman' stood in the way, for he was opposed to me in politics. He kept me calling in expectation day after day till every web was gone, and then, with a fiendish sneer, he told me to 'go and live on the Charter.' I need not, because I cannot, tell the sad effects of this terrible disappointment on our family; but when I looked into my poor father's pale face and upon his hungry ones around me, my first impulse was vengeance on this monster in human form. But the time-serving fellow not being within my reach, and my not being in possession of the necessary physical strength to chastise him, I only asked in bitterness,

'Why has man the will and power
To make his fellow mourn?'

"I so far forgot myself and God that I became enraged. Whence have come this deep wrong—dear bread, want of work, this hungry and roused nation? I asked myself, as I thought of the wickedness of the strong and the wretchedness of the weak. And viewing things from my limited point of observation—while suffering the fearful results of what I could not but regard as a galling injustice—I felt the growing power of the conviction that all who had lost all sense of justice were supported in their iniquitous dealings by those in authority. Such was the influence of such doings and thoughts that I became almost ready to kick against *all* authority, as a stronghold of all that was base and debasing, as a terror to the sufferer, and a protection to the treacherous, as the enemy of God and goodness, the friend of vice and villany. So strong did this conviction become that, at times, when very hungry and failing to get work, I felt as if I would make mince-pie of all the M.P.'s.

"But, in justice to myself—and, no doubt, speaking for many others like myself—I must add, there was nothing of what may be properly called malice in my heart. Personally, I knew not *one* in authority whom I wished to be even unseated. My whole soul went out against the *whole system*, in consequence of what was happening in the nation at large, as well as in the village at home. Such thoughts were purely the result of hunger and insult, torment and misery. But they were very dangerous and very prevalent, the fuel for the fire, the suppressed smoke ready to burst into flame. To me they were very injurious, putting away every source of comfort and consolation, driving God and goodness out of the soul."

AT A HUNGRY GATHERING.

Surely this confession—coupled as it is with his wail of woe—is worthy of the notice of the philanthropist, if not the statesman and divine. It shows what one may be driven to, and one of whom it was afterwards said—"In him all the charities and genialities and homely sympathies of human nature find free and unfettered play, a glow of a high moral purpose pervading his life."

And there was what followed when, with him as with others, all that was sad rose to a fearful crisis—he being led from one step to another, and each becoming worse. What between his Secretaryship, writing paragraphs, preparing and delivering speeches, he had plenty of work, but "nothing for it." He tells us, too, that "the excitement was so great, and at times the fun (?) was such that one would not have wearied during these otherwise sadly dull times; but hunger would not keep away, and precious time was passing on."

At last, however, he was so far misled—and that contrary to the advice of his suffering, sorrowing father—as to be induced to join a "hungry mob" in their "pilgrimage of folly" from Dundee to Forfar and back. During that journey he heard some curious addresses and saw strange things. The following is one of the "heroic stamp" of the speeches which he himself has placed on record, and at which he now laughs most heartily. Before the gathering entered Forfar one of the "orators" said:—

"Dear Fellowmen—We are here an' there maun be nae flinchin'. Hunger has brocht us here, fellowmen, an' we maun do our wark. I hae lookit lang for the cause of our poverty; I hae lookit for it at our ain hames, an' canna get it there—there is nae great livin' there. I hae lookit to the sky aboon, to the sun, an' the stars, an' the moon, an' dinna see it there. Na, na, fellowmen, there is nae misery there. The sun has dun its work, an' there's the clear moon makin' the corn ripe afore ye. But I hae also lookit up to the big house o' Parliament, in Lundin, an' hae found it there. Yes, fellowmen! yes, it is there, I assure ye. It is their falt, they hae been makin' bad laws, an' takin' athing to theirsels, an' makin' us hungry here. An' fat is far waur, fellowmen, there is nane wrocht an' starved like the folk a' Scotland here; an' fu sud we starve in a land o' plenty? Na, fellowmen, na! we maun do our best. Sae up, fellowmen! there maun be nae flinchin' noo. The Charter, an' no surrender!"— Tremendous cheers, and a flourish of branches.

But whatever the leaders said, and whatever they intended to do, it is only fair to give our young "Rebel's" own explanation in the matter, so far as he is concerned. Referring to this "turn-out," he says, "Though it may appear foolish—as foolish it was—I went to do I knew not what; and I verily believe many of those who joined us were in the same position."

Still this "Trip to Forfar" did not mend matters. It made them much worse for him.

CHAPTER IV.

ON THE TRAMP.

NO WHERE TO LAY HIS HEAD.

No prospect of anything to do, and having no hope of being helpful to his father and the family, he made up his mind to leave home in search of work. Introducing the reader to what follows, he remarks, "Some one has truly said, that 'a man willing to work and unable to find that work, is perhaps the saddest sight that Fortune's inequalities exhibit under the sun. It *is* truly a sad sight to see a man begging a brother of the earth to give him leave to toil.' But when man solicits in vain, and can neither find food nor shelter, the aspect is even sadder. But surely the saddest sight of all is when the poor wanderer is young and weak, and has in him those strong emotions which bespeak an aspiring soul."

It was, we believe, about this time that the loom of the Inverary poet, William Thoms, was silenced at Newtyle, and that he, too, had to start on those adventures which his genius has made immortal. But though the wanderings of Mr Hillocks were of another stamp, they are equally interesting and more instructive. We shall give them in his own words, because in the ungarnished description of his condition he waxes pathetic, and at times he is poetical. We shall break in where he says, "I endured much before I got steady employment, but I shall only give one of the many instances of suffering during my sad sojourning.

"Reduced to one penny, I left Montrose for Brechin. The rich smile of fading day gilded the big tears of all but despair as they rolled down my pale cheeks. For a time I stood still and wept bitterly, and was all the better for it. Hope, as a dim shadow, appeared, and I plodded on till the last rays of the great orb of day had vanished, and the 'wee stars' began to run their path through the sky. All was hushed—it was a thrilling hush. Profound silence remained unmolested save the sharp beating within my breast, the rapidity of which increased as the road before me and all around me grew more dreary.

"I was faint as well as afraid, but I plodded along till a darting pang of hunger brought me down. Such are these pangs, the keenness of which can only be known to those who have felt them. Being very hungry before I left Montrose, I had bought some ginger-bread with my only penny, but I could not eat more than the half of it; and I had not been far on my way before I met a beggar woman and some children, all of whom seemed to be as much in want as I was, so they had my store.

"But God did not leave me, though I had sometimes left Him. He was kind. He did not then send bread, because then I could not eat it; but He sent sleep, that which I so much wanted. When I was in this all but insensible state, Nature's soft nurse threw her gentle arms around me, and wafted my soul to the land of dreams. It was a glorious dream, but only a dream. Imagine my surprise when I awoke and found myself, where I had folded my weary limbs, upon the hard bedewed wayside. Again my heart and spirit almost failed me as I felt bewildered; but as soon as I could walk I continued my journey to Brechin, arriving there in the morning.

"There I found the poor weaver to whom I had a note of introduction. He did not mention breakfast—perhaps he had not any himself—and I could not ask it. It was hard times in Brechin, too, and there was no hope for me there; but our meeting was not in vain—it was a link in the mysterious chain of a loving Providence."

HOW THE POOR HELP THE POOR.

Though he did not get work at Brechin he procured another note of introduction to a weaver at Luthermuir—a semi-hamlet and semi-village lying in a flat plain about seven miles east of Brechin, and nine miles north of Montrose. About this time—1842 or 1843—the inhabitants were almost entirely weavers. Since then they have been increased by a strong admixture of Irish navvies. It was a miserable place; yet, to our hero, it seemed a "happy haven." His account of his first entrance is a page of real interest. He says:—

"By the time I reached the man to whom my introductory note was addressed, my legs could scarcely bear me up. I fell asleep in his house before food could be got ready for me. When I awoke I was kindly offered some bread and a cup of tea; but, being so hungry and fatigued, I could not eat, becoming very faint, so much so that the kind people thought I had died. As I recovered somewhat, I heard one say—'Poor fellow! perhaps he has not tasted food the day before.' This was too true, for I had eaten nothing save the half of my penny cake of ginger-bread for thirty hours.

"But while I was receiving this hearty sympathy and kind hospitality from my humane 'hostess' and her generous neighbours, my equally obliging 'host' was out to the village agents inquiring what news from Montrose, whence he and the others were longing for work. I was not a little astonished at the careworn and anxious-looking appearance of those around me, but as the host entered, he solved the problem. His countenance caused every one to smile; and every one leaped for

joy when he, addressing me, exclaimed in an animated tone—
'Guid news the nicht, min! cheer up; there's twa cart-load o' wabs come, an' every one has gotten a wab, an' there's twa to spare for you; there has nae been the like o' this for sax months afore.' I was happy to see others so glad, and said that I would be grateful if I could get a web to-morrow. 'There's nae fear o' us noo,' said a female from the neighbourhood, in a joyful tone; 'God's to be good to us again.' 'Amen,' said I, 'and may He reward you for your kind attention to me. Perhaps I'll be the better for coming here.' 'I hope so,' responded a sensible middle-aged man, as he was bidding me good-night. 'You know,' said he, very seriously yet smilingly, 'all places that the eye of Heaven visits are to a wise man ports and happy havens.'

"It was after the neighbours had retired that the most searching questions were put, drawing from me some idea of what I had undergone. It is said the *real* Scotchman would always be independent, if possible—that he would almost sooner starve than beg—and I confess I was touched with this spirit; but on this occasion I endeavoured to strike out a middle course—that is, to reveal as little as possible of my past sufferings, and yet to give a reason for my sad condition. This reason was not necessary to lead to help. The help had been rendered. Without any questions, my new friends had proved themselves to be in possession of no small share of the milk of human kindness. They did more than they were able. They had the heart and the will, and that helped them to find the way, though they were nearly as poor as myself.

"I could not help asking myself, what would the poor do were it not for the poor?"

SUCCESS, AND THE RETURN HOME.

"But this was not all. Others soon manifested a like kindness. In a few days I began to gather strength, and was soon able to ask for work. In this I succeeded, to the joy of all who had heard of 'the new tramp.' But when I received my first web I did not know very well how to go to work, the fabric being so very fine compared with that to which I had been accustomed. Pressing necessity caused me to venture, but I was not long left in the dilemma. As soon as my shopmates observed it, they came to the rescue, rendering all necessary help without being asked. I got on so well that I was soon able to make as good work and wages as any in the place."

Willing to work and having plenty of work is a great source of happiness to such workmen as our friend has ever been. Hence he was glad, even in this out-of-the-way place. We shall not soon forget the fact that "twa cart fu' o' wabs" made a whole village rejoice, and that one of the men thus made happy is found quoting fine English poetry in token of gratitude.

Continuing the record, the "young weaver" adds—"At the end of one month, I was able to get some clothes to make me respectable; at the end of the second month, I was able to send some help to my dear father; and at the end of the third month, I returned home, healthy, happy, and thankful."

A POINT GAINED.

Well may he ask, "What would the poor do were it not for the poor?" This is a very suggestive question, and the simple narration of this touching episode shows what the poor can do for the poor—here their great kindness turned the ebbing tide in the life of one who could not have withstood the terrible buffetings of adversity much longer. In this out-of-the-way place he saw much that he would have wished otherwise; but he felt the force and the benefit of practical charity, and this made him afterwards give a kind word on behalf of such, and to which we shall refer in due course. The society of many of the "tramps of Luthermuir" was not so pure, and therefore not so pleasant, as our young "tramp" would have wished; but he was careful to do all the good he could, and to store up all the good he could find. Nor was he without his "transporting moments," arising from profitable contemplations and the enjoyment of pleasing sights and delightful sounds seen and heard during his morning and evening walks in the woods and fields. "I cannot," he says, "find words to express the joy which I felt when listening to the crow of the cock in his gaiety, the whirring of the pheasant as he sprung from the break, the song of the lark as he soared to meet the rising day, the chatter of the swallow as she plied her dappled wings along the crystal streamlet, and the hum of the busy insect as it sipped the dew-drop from the opening flower."

And this joyousness he carried with him to the village hut which he has described. "Home, home, sweet home, there is no place like home," was the refrain which occupied his mind as he returned to his former "study" under the thatched roof of this poor abode. He says he did not regret the journey in search of work, after that journey was finished and blessed. "The beginning was bitter, but the end was sweet," and he was thankful. It is true, from the scholastic aspect, there was not much advancement, yet he learned much that has been useful to him. And then he was enabled to return full of new life and fresh vigour, resolving to lay aside the further consideration of politics, and almost every other matter not educational.

Being fortunate to receive plenty of work from what was the foundation of the well-known firm, Cox Brothers, he was soon able to purchase more books, and ere long he was seen at his old "desk" pursuing his studies with anxious care—continuing his "struggles to learn"—always at the evening classes, and occasionally at the day-school as before—making such rapid progress till, at last, he became an Assistant Teacher.

But even this was not enough for one whose motto was, and still is, "Excelsior." He continued to press "onward and upward"—weaving, and learning, and teaching—in the hope of one day becoming the "Principal of some Academy."

And that day came. He says, "When the proper time arrived, I sold my loom in Lochee and rented an empty house at Smithfield, top of Hilltown, Dundee. There, on the 25th of November, 1844, I opened my first public school."

CHAPTER V.

THRICE SAVED ON ONE SUNDAY.

HAVING accompanied our friend thus far, perhaps it is well, at this point, to retrace our steps. Incidents not a few, and thoughts not to be slighted, cluster round the natural and important question—"What was the spiritual experience of our friend while struggling to live and learn under such trying hardships?" This experience is incidentally alluded to in "Life Story," and we understand that he has promised to his friends, the late Thomas Guthrie of Edinburgh, and the late Thomas Binney of London, to give a more detailed account of this as soon as his other duties permitted him; but, as the subject is very interesting, we cannot altogether overlook it here. The inner life is even more important than the outer life, more especially in this case, and specially to the young who may read these pages. Therefore, we shall as briefly as possible bring before the reader a few of the "all things" which he assures us "God was pleased to bless and work together for good." And the first, in point of date, is what he has called—" Thrice saved on one Sunday."

ABOUT TO SINK IN THE DEEP.

He truly remarks that "one of the sad consequences of poverty is this: its victims are frequently compelled to live in the midst of much that is offensive to the eye, the ear, and the mind of the honest poor." Adding, "To my parents' grief, the most of the children as well as their parents in our neighbourhood were very wicked. Often did they try to induce me to join them in their Sunday journeys, and once they were successful.

"One Sunday forenoon, before my father left for Divine Service, he, as was his wont, enjoined us not to leave home. We promised obedience, and we meant to obey. However, he was not long gone, when I was enticed by some boys in the passage to speak to them. This was the starting-point. I possessed a halfpenny, and very foolishly, though naturally, exhibited my store to those around me. This excited their cupidity, and increased their anxiety to get me with them. By an eloquence worthy of a better cause, they led me on, and by a thousand wiles tried to get my halfpenny.

"At last they led me to the harbour, nearly two miles distant from our home, and offered me a sail in a boat moored to the steps which led to the water. This offer I accepted, but promised to pay only after I had the sail.

"Their intention was to let me out the length of the rope, and then pull the boat back to the steps. But one of the boys present was stronger and more wicked than the rest, and, having no interest at stake, he pulled the rope from them and threw it into the water. The result was I was soon drifting helplessly out with the tide, and was approaching some of the most dangerous places, when—almost paralysed with terror—I was picked up by some men, who, seeing my danger, had made haste to the rescue. A policeman was ready to seize me when I landed. He laid hold of me and threatened much, but I told my simple story, and he let me off with a harshly-uttered warning and a very hard kick—both of which I took with the best possible grace, and ran off thankful that I had escaped a watery grave."

WHIRLING IN THE AIR.

"The boys with whom I had bargained had run at the approach of the policeman, but as soon as they saw I was clear off, they made up to me and demanded the fare. I could not see it was proper to pay for being nearly drowned, so I kept my halfpenny, and made for home. But when I arrived at the top of the lane which led to our house, I was afraid to go further. By this time the people were returning from public worship, and, in order that my father might not see me, I went beyond the lane. This afforded a favourable opportunity for the boys with whom I had left home. They followed me, and strange to say, I kept to the bad company—or they to me—like the drunkard to his glass.

"Though young, I was able to reason somewhat; at least I knew I had done wrong in breaking my promise to a kind father and going so far astray. And yet in this state of anxiety—and with good resolutions in my mind—I did not then return, but went still further away. At last we came to an entrance to a field, in which a large number of very rough carters were grazing their horses.

"What a scene! I think I see it yet. Some of the men were sleeping on the grass, some were drinking, some were dead drunk, some were fighting, some were playing at cards, others at pitch-and-toss; and almost all who could open their mouths were cursing, as a matter of course. I learned afterwards that this was the fearful way in which these men passed their Sundays during the summer months.

"From childhood I admired the grand and beautiful in nature and art wherever I saw them; here my eyes were fixed on the horses, many of which were the opposite of handsome; but among them was one beauty, and upon it I fixed my eyes in admiration. My mind must have been filled with such thoughts as spring into being when contemplating the graphic and glowing description of the horse in the book of Job. The lovely creature on which I feasted my eyes was called 'Missie.' She had just been banished to the cart because of her 'vices.' Her owner had been gambling, and had lost all. Glad of even a halfpenny, that he might try his luck once more, and having heard of mine, he offered me a ride on 'Missie' if I would give the copper to him. Fascinated with the beautiful animal, I consented. Greatly delighted, but very timid, I was helped upon her back, but he gave her such a smart cut with the whip, that in a moment I was thrown whirling in the air, so high that those who were looking on did not expect to pick me up alive, fearing my neck would be broken by the fall."

HANGING ON A PRECIPICE.

"Though I was much hurt—but not nearly so much as was feared—I made my way home as soon as I could creep along, supporting myself by resting my hand against the low dyke or wall which bounded the field on the road-side. Some of the boys followed me, and, by their advice, we took what they called a near cut, and when we approached the 'braes,' that is, the cliffs, by the side of the river, one of the lads threw a stone from the top of the cliff. This startled and vexed a soldier, who, with his sweetheart, was reclining on the slope below. Of course he must be gallant, so he made charge after us. My companions were about as fleet as he was, but I, fatigued and crippled, was unable to follow them. As I could not run from the red-coated fury, I contrived to dodge; and, in my extremity, I crept behind a furze bush near to one of the rocky precipices. But, imagine my fear, just as he passed me I began to slip down. Perceiving my danger, I called out for assistance; but on the soldier went, still in pursuit. Now, almost at the very brink, clinging to the slippery grass, I again called out as for life. Another moment, thought I, and I am gone to pay the penalty of Sabbath desecration.

"But I was barefooted, and the old root of a bush was placed so that my toes entered into the bend; and thus I was enabled to support myself, holding desperately by the grass with my hands till the soldier returned. He, with no small risk and by considerable ingenuity, succeeded in bringing me once more to the pathway.

"To him I also told all that had come to pass to me that day, and he wept, even before his sweetheart, who by this time had joined us. Seeing this proof of tender-heartedness, I thought he might become an effective advocate, and asked him to accompany me home to intercede for me, as my father was certain to be sorely vexed because of my leaving home, and that in bad company. He complied with my request, and I had no occasion to speak. He told the day's adventures as I had related them to him.

"My parents were grieved because of what I had done; but glad I had been spared and brought home. So was I, and never did I forget that Sunday—never did I thank God more heartily for delivering me—saving me from the jaws of death, into which I had run through disobedience.

"'Thrice saved in one day!' said I to myself. Surely for some good purpose. Though I saw in all this the hand of God *only as a poor but repentant child could see it*, yet I felt *He* had preserved me, and I loved Him more than ever."

CHAPTER VI.

THINGS WORKING TOGETHER FOR GOOD.

IN course of time these three thrilling incidents were followed by others equally useful, each in their own way. We select a few. Speaking from experience, he tells us that "a kind word from a good friend is often greatly blessed. My parents," he adds, "were frequently visited by their minister, and I soon became his pet. Due reverence was paid to the good man and his high calling. However hard-up we were, and pressed for time, all work was suspended during his stay, and this gave me the opportunity of drawing nearer and nearer to him, until he took me between his knees and held my hand while he talked or listened. He did not come to overawe us because of his position, nor to frighten us by hard questions, but to give us good advice in a cheerful manner. He also tried to direct the conversation so as to lead my father on to the narration of incidents connected with storms or battles in which he had taken an active part. And from the simple sketches thus given by the poor tar, this eloquent preacher would paint in glowing language some grand or terrible picture which often served as thrilling introductions to his sermons."

This minister, we understand, was George Donaldson, one of our predecessors in our pastorate, and it must be cheering to his friends yet living to know how his kind words have been blessed where perhaps they little thought. How he won this young soul is thus told:—"After a few cheering words to all around, he would place his left hand softly upon my head and gently press up my chin with the half-bent forefinger of the right hand until my eyes would meet his smiling face, and then he would tell me how I might yet be a good man, and perhaps a minister, too. And, though he has long since gone to glory, the influence of his kindly encouragement continues to grow, still producing good fruit. I can see in him the blessed example of the Master, who not only said, 'Suffer the children to come unto Me,' but who also put his hands on them and blessed them. Truly, this valuable minister drew me closer to 'The Children's Friend.' If well-meaning ladies and gentlemen only knew the valuable influence of kind attention towards poor depressed children, surely kind words and kind acts would be more numerous."

THE SUNDAY SCHOOL.

The truth of this remark is also seen in another of the means of grace specially blessed in connection with one of the most useful institutions of our day.

See the lad in his new suit of Sunday clothes—the result of unrelenting perseverance and hard work. This "Anxious Inquirer" is on his way to the Sunday-school. And we are glad to learn that this step was taken in accordance with an advice given by us at the close of a sermon preached to the young on the previous Sunday; the advice being that all present not attending the Sunday-school should do so as soon as possible.

As he entered the school, a strange chill—arising from an indescribable emotion—came over him, but fortunately the good Superintendent came forward to the bashful boy, and, with one of those very pleasing and winning smiles, for which he is so well-known in Dundee, kindly put the usual questions —placing the timid boy in a suitable class.

D

This good friend is our worthy townsman, David Robertson, of Union Grove, the able and energetic President of our Young Men's Christian Association, which is doing so much to meet the spiritual and intellectual wants of Dundee. Many are very thankful to Mr Robertson for his kindly care in each of their individual cases, but none are more grateful to him and thankful to God than Mr Hillocks is, not only for the timely kindness rendered, but also for the happy results which have continued to flow on since the Sunday on which he entered the Mid-Wynd Sunday-school. In his little book entitled, "The Sabbath-school from a practical point of view," which he dedicated to Mr Robertson, he says, he owes some of the sweetest and endearing associations, stirring gratitude in his heart and giving joy to his soul. "The family altar," he truly says, "is pleasant and profitable—may it soon be erected in every home—but the Sunday-school is needed, especially for those who have not the blessed opportunity of bending and learning at that sacred altar; I mean the children of the outcast and the children of the careless. They may not read of the kind invitation of Jesus in the precious Word, but they may hear of it—as thousands have heard of it for the first time, from the lips of a devoted Sunday-school teacher. I thank God I heard it; and the joy it produced is yet fresh in my mind. The Sunday-school greatly assisted me to

'Behold the best, the greatest gift of everlasting love.'"

USEFUL TRACTS.

And associated with this was the reading of some useful tracts. The nursery books to which he had referred served their purpose for the time. He says, "Never did I love the Robin so fondly till I read how kindly he covered the poor babes with the forest leaves. And even yet, although I love all birds and enjoy their varied song, I confess the sight of the Redbreast brings up a loving feeling stronger than that which I experience in beholding any other of the feathered tribe." But this was not enough. The taste for reading being acquired, it grew with the opportunity. Having a good voice, he became the family reader as time permitted. On the Sunday he might have been seen, surrounded by the family and some of the neighbours, reading the religious tracts he had gathered during the week. And such was the benefit derived from this exercise, that it not only fostered piety in the family and those who frequently assembled with them, it was often blessed to his own soul, "refreshing and invigorating" his mind. This accounts for his warm praise of good tracts, enforcing his opinion as to their usefulness by the aid of the following appropriate quotation from William Howett, slightly altered, we think:—"Tracts run up and down like the angels of God, blessing all, giving to all, and asking no gift in return. They can be printed in all sizes, on all subjects, in all places, at all hours. They can talk to one as well as to a multitude, and to a multitude as well as one. They can tell their story in the kitchen or the shop, in the parlour or the closet, in the railway carriage or the omnibus, on the broad highway or in the footpath through the field; and no one can betray them into hasty or random expressions. Being short and to the point, they may thus speak wisely and well, and so become the teachers and reformers of all classes, the regenerators and benefactors of all lands." He adds, "A good tract, having the blessing of the Divine Master, often becomes the messenger of mercy; it may rouse a country to a sense of its duty, shaking the foundations of corruption; or it may tell, as it often tells, the good news as proclaimed in the simple and blessed Gospel of Jesus Christ, as it did to me, renewing and confirming what I had previously heard and read."

WHAT SOME BOOKS DID FOR HIM.

Of necessity he was a lad of few books. This we see from the catalogue he has given us, but there are others which have not yet been specially mentioned, and which did much for him. He says, "I had longed for a book about Sir William Wallace; and at last I got a copy of Blind Harry's quaint rhymes on the remarkable deeds of the great hero. How I devoured this interesting book! The good aim, the earnest patriotism, the mighty strength of the overpowering chief wrought like a charm upon my mind, and before I had gone through the book, I felt the full force of the poet's words—

> 'At Wallace's name, what Scottish blood,
> But boils up in a spring-tide flood?'"

As for Burns, he continues, "How I read and laughed, and wept! I earnestly wished that I might be able to evince even a tenth part of his vast, rich, and glowing genius. There was such a charm about him that I was almost falling in love with all he said and did, even with his errors. There was also something in my circumstances at the time which made me most ready to swallow his bitter things. Happily ere this, I had experienced the religious feelings so eloquently, graphically, and touchingly expressed in his "Cottar's Saturday Night;" but I had seen a specimen of, and had suffered from, the hypocrisy which quailed under his withering, under his cutting satire. I admired, nay, almost worshipped the poet, but wept for the man.

"And as for the Scottish Worthies," he adds, "their manly and heroic deeds, their strong hearts and noble aims, their indomitable resolution, and wild enthusiasm, stamped an impression upon my mind that will ever remain. Their glorious deeds won my admiration, and their intense sufferings awakened my sympathy. Often did I pause and tremble when reading the stirring records of these stern and savage times. What a glorious idea, thought I to myself, to see the rich and poor, the learned and unlettered, asserting the right to think for themselves, rising in fearless honesty against oppression, and bravely vindicating, to the death, the liberty of the human conscience—to see them manfully paying the stern penalty of their burning love towards eternal truth! to see them—

'Still pressing onward, red-wat-shod,'

to victory or death; and at last dying in hope and in the sweet peace of believing!"

And the same enthusiasm is manifested in reference to Bunyan's best book. He says, "The beautiful and inspiring story of the 'Pilgrim's Progress' was of another stamp, but no less interesting. Tell a boy in his teens that this book is a work of fiction, and he will not readily believe you. There is such a reality about it. But it becomes doubly interesting to the youth if he has, by God's help, commenced his homeward, the heavenly journey. To him the great allegory becomes a great fact—a splendid conception, admirably illustrated by the life of the noble Pilgrim himself—a book alike for old and young, and for all conditions and positions in life."

And it is proper to add that the Book of books was his book. Other books were useful to him, but it was at the fountain of all truth, the Word of God, that his heart was refreshed and his soul strengthened—especially when "imbibing the Gospels, learning the words and ways of Jesus." He says, "The joy and profit which I derived from the sacred pages cannot be described. Though I could in a measure (only as a boy could) see the soundness of its maxims, the wisdom of its precepts, and the importance of its commands, yet to me its poetry was more attractive than its philosophy; and its history, its journeys, and biographies, gained from me more time than its prophecies and doctrines. I felt such a pleasure in drinking deeper and deeper at this blessed fountain. I cannot tell the grateful emotions which filled my heart as I found in the Divine Book lessons so suited to my age, and instruction so well adapted to my condition. With a hearty enthusiasm, and the tears of gratitude streaming down my pale cheeks, I was able to join in the sentiment of the hymn, beginning—

'Holy Bible, book divine,
　Precious treasure, thou art mine.'"

CHAPTER VII.

THE DAWN DARKENED.

THE LIGHT OBSCURED.

"Thus it was," as he says, "that God was pleased to work all things together for good. I loved my Father in Jesus, and the Comforter blessed my soul." But, alas! he in time, for a season, fell into the troubled waters of religious doubt, and became fearfully unsettled. This need not be a matter of surprise, though it is greatly to be regretted, not more on his account than on the account of others who have also fallen—and some are falling even now—by the same or similar causes. The more immediate results of these causes vary in various intellects and temperaments, under various degrees of culture and kinds of circumstances, but there is an evident similarity running through them all. Still, some are more generally felt than others. What injured our friend in a very special manner might not have been known, or, at least, noticed by others moving in another sphere of life; the circumstances as well as the training being different.

In his case—having an observing eye and a sensitive mind—the foundation of this Doubting Castle was laid by the conduct, or rather the misconduct of some professors of religion known to him. It is truly pitiful to read his thrilling wail. In one part he says:—" By the grace of God, when I was yet of tender years, I was enabled, by the eye of simple faith, to see the day-star arise. Though, to me, that beautiful star seemed then to be far, far away—"like a diamond in the sky"—yet I believed as well as wondered. Though often greatly depressed, because of much suffering, yet in God I was glad. Believing *He* was good, and wise, and loving, I could trust Him, though I could not trace Him. But, alas! at last, that confidence was sadly shaken, and my happiness greatly marred. I was unwilling to offend God, and yet I was conscious of wandering from Him.

"In my distress I wept and prayed, but my faith was so weak that I became afraid it was unbelief. I would have all Christians to be like Christ, and I felt I was not like Him, and I saw so many very *unlike* Him. Dread filled my soul—a terrible fear lest I, too, might become like many I saw around me without faith, hope, and charity, though they named the name of Jesus."

Think of him, poor lad, hard driven by the world and uncharitably spoken of by not a few who "named the name of Jesus." True, all were not alike; some professed believers meant to be kind, but even they so unwisely managed matters that they seemed to have in view the *burning* out of his young doubts by the strongest of caustic, instead of healing them by the Balm of Gilead. He says:—"Timid though I was, I ventured to speak to one or two whom I thought might help to keep me in the way; but they did not understand me; they seemed as dark as I was, as if they knew nothing of the thoughts that troubled me. They could give no reason for the faith by which they professed to be guided, and the interpretations they put on various passages of Scripture I could not reconcile with the wise and loving character of God, which I had entertained and cherished."

Here was a subject for the kindly care of our Young Men's Christian Associations. What great suffering might have been saved had our young friend been brought under a better treatment, a milder and more humane mode of dealing with young men's understandings, consciences, and hearts. Finding he could not be driven, he was left alone, as if he had no soul to feed; but not long, for others—some of whom had been soured by the same causes which estranged him—sought his presence. Neglected by the professedly religious, he was the easier induced to frequent the company of those who made no profession of religion. Speaking of them, he says, "They soon became very anxious to get me advanced (?) to their standard, and for that purpose they lent me their books, some of which possessed an intellectual grandeur which I could not but admire, whilst their profuse glitter confused me more than ever. Unwilling to leave Christ, I cried for help, for I found the frightful conviction growing stronger and stronger—that what was called Christianity was not divine, because I could not see its influence for good on the minds and conduct of those who professed to be actuated by its principles and guided by its precepts. But I was not willing to allow this to rest as a settled conviction. I felt, or rather desired to feel, that it was erroneous; but this fact stared me in the face, namely, that with very few exceptions those with whom I had met who professed to be religious were anything but loving and loveable, anything but honest and charitable, anything but what they tried to make others believe they were. To me, the majority seemed to be God's children *by pretension* for the fifty-two Sundays of each year, and the devil's *by practice* for the remaining three hundred and thirteen days. All this, and the fact of the great national suffering existing—which I regarded as the result of political and social wrong, a result which I thought should not have been known in a Christian country —confirmed my rather hastily drawn conclusion, and led me farther astray."

A WORD ON BEHALF OF YOUNG MEN.

Most people will readily admit that it is greatly to be deplored that such a child-like faith should be so shaken as to take away almost all purely spiritual joy, and yet we live in the midst of such causes as led to the doubt and the absence of happiness of our young friend; causes even deeper and more dangerous than those he has named, and because of which many of our youth of all classes have been wandering to all the Albanas and Pharpars within their reach, instead of to the streams of Jordan and Silva's soft flowing waters. Now, as then, these stumbling-blocks are in the way, obstructing the healthy progress of the most earnest and the best of young doubters. As we shall see, *they* make many mistakes, not being always able to form a correct judgment, often placing themselves as between two fires; but with blame pity should come. They, like our young friend, frequently take their stand by the words, "By their fruits ye shall know them"—meaning the creeds and those who profess them—and this is a good standard, if not perverted. Some young doubters may be able to admit that the working of certain narrow forms of belief, may, in some cases, help to keep men from gross sin; but this does not increase nor strengthen *their* faith. They may see that from under these forms of belief have sprung some fine developments of Christian character; but, say they, such instances have generally been seen in those who were naturally of a noble type, who became strong enough to burst the fetters of narrow thought—and then they are carried away with what is too true, that the conduct is seldom regulated by what is often best in such creeds, in many cases not even modified. They see where there is zeal, it is too often zeal without knowledge, the zeal of the bigots, madly in love with their own party, fiercely opposed to most others.

All that and all its consequences are very productive of scepticism, especially when any of the leaders in religious thought are suspicious of Art, Literature, and Philosophy, uncharitable in their judgments, injurious in their language, implacable in their animosities, ferocious in their anathemas, believing that they, their party, and a few other parties scattered through the world, are from God, and that all the rest of mankind, and nature herself, are from the devil. Not that they say this in so many words, but they act as if they believed it. And the sad effects of all this tell more powerfully if it is seen in those who have been trained under what is called "the ministry"—as is generally the case where the ministers have been either sternly cold or haughtily silent in matters pertaining to that which is human and humane—where the most startling statements have been pronounced with the utmost emphasis, sometimes with fury, accompanied by damnatory denunciations, and that not always by men most conspicuous for their virtue or benevolence. Where this is the case, we need not be surprised if earnest young men stagger as they contrast the statements of the Bible with the practice of those who profess to take it as a lamp to their feet and a light to their path. We have admitted that young men often consider such things, statements, and conduct when in a state of mind unsuited to the work; but then they are driven to it, whether able or unable. Strong statements and inconsistent conduct challenge investigation; and sensitive souls, wincing under a deep sense of wrong, naturally look at the forms of creeds with the sharp, and, sometimes, with the untrained eye of youthful distrust. And, as it not unfrequently happens, they see, or think they see, in the creeds they "examine" much that is very terrible, even if it were true; much that is very withering, very hopeless, as well as very mysterious. They find, or think they find, that much of what is being so dogmatically pronounced as true is founded on far less than demonstrative evidence. Their disgust deepens, and often Christianity is given up.

This is very sad, but let us rejoice that even in its midst—as in the case of our friend—there are some who burst the limiting or fettering obstacles and attain the Christian form of noble manhood. But, alas! for one who rises, many stumble and fall, some to scatter broadcast the seed which has destroyed their own peace of mind and lessened their usefulness. Generally the confused souls either halt between two opinions and become mere nonentities, or go off at a tangent of total defiance and opposition to the views of their friends. And when this is the case, the falling away generally acts injuriously on their moral nature, if not on their habits of life.

While most determinedly opposed to all the licentiousness and dogmatism generally associated with one-sided scepticism, we plead that a more thoughtful kindness be manifested towards young men, those of them who are honest doubters, that each individual case, with the various surroundings and training, be carefully considered. Only conceive of young men full of love—and the glories of science and literature rising round them like autumnal stars—surrounded by an atmosphere, the chief element of which being intolerable exclusiveness and narrow partyism! Surely it would be better for young men, for the Church, and hence for the world—at least, it would indicate greater wisdom and a better heart—were the leaders of religious thought to consider what would serve as a counteractive to speculation.

True, it has happened that there has been a falling away even when the young men were thoroughly satisfied with the good faith, real talent, and undoubted excellence of the preacher. Thus Theodore Parker sat for long under Dr Beecher's ministry—his reverence for the man, and his determined aversion to his doctrine increasing at the same rate from year to year. Yet we feel convinced that if kindly dealing with young inquirers was the rule there would be less young doubt, or at least, what doubt did exist would all the sooner pass away to be exchanged for a more enlarged, and therefore more solid and lasting form of faith. Certainly there would be less obscuring of the light; the dawn would not be so often darkened. Our young men would be more useful; and, therefore, happier.

YOUNG MEN'S MISTAKES.

But while we deeply deplore the existence of so much that is unreal, so hollow, as well as erroneous; while we know that such is among the causes of youthful scepticism, we must also be faithful to those whom we pity, and for whom we plead. We must frankly tell young men that they, too, in their often inconsiderate zeal, make many and sad mistakes. They too often forget what has been already indicated—and which has been again and again clearly proved—that circumstances in life and the condition of the mind may, to a certain extent, unfit a young man for judging as fully and impartially as is desirable. And yet how frequently many of them speak as with authority—in the very same dogmatism of which they so loudly complain—rashly and often harshly assailing all around, often beginning with the pulpit. Now we hold that every minister of the Gospel should be on the side of whatever tends to the spread of practical Christianity; but we are anxious to discourage all indiscriminate blame, because those aggrieved are not always in a position to make the just and necessary allowances. The minister sees difficulties which are not known to those who complain. And these difficulties are often of such a nature as only a few dare venture to overleap. And, besides, on the other side, there are other people—not necessarily the rich nor the poor—who are too frequently watching the minister; while many of such are sure, on the first opportunity, to bring home to him the ever-ready charge of meddling with politics. And, then, may he not be sincere in the belief that if he adopted another course than that taken, he might thereby have hindered his general and greater usefulness?

And we admit what has often been said—and it is truly lamentable that there is even a shadow of truth in it—that the part which the ministers of religion take, whether silent or active, is generally regarded by the poor as adverse to their interest and comfort. It cannot be denied that too many of the clergy have pooh-poohed, or strongly denounced popular movements—often trying to trace them to the perversity of human nature; whereas, in the main, they have been the necessary advance of the intellect of the age. It will be well for the Church, and hence for the world, when the leaders in religious matters try to kindly regulate, instead of rudely check, that which demands public attention. At present there are no such deep currents of political feeling running now as when the very unfavourable impressions were being made on the mind of our young friend; yet these may come again, and besides, at all times there are motives of mind and tendencies of thought in all ranks, in the high as well as the low, to which the attitude of the clergy has become a matter of great importance. But all only shows the necessity of honest doubters bearing in mind that all have duties, personal and relative, and their duty is to be more careful lest they arrive at too hasty conclusions in regard to what may be the sincere belief and honest purpose of others.

And this caution is needful in regard to the words and ways of those in the pew as well as those in the pulpit. We admit there is a fearful laxity of morals in *all* classes—a laxity which owes its existence greatly to the increasing luxury of the manner and mode of living; a laxity which carries many on in the errors of their way, until they, in large numbers, are found sharing in that extraordinary unsettlement of thought which is the peculiarity of the age, where all is seething fermentation, where everything old has been cast into the furnace, and it is as yet uncertain how much is to come out and how much is to be consumed. But this is a proof that all who court serious thought and free expression should consider their personal responsibility and probable influence.

Again, I admit there is nothing more natural than to expect to see proofs of a Christian life in those who profess to follow Christ. When the life and creed agree, it is a valuable subsidiary proof of the sincerity of the one and the truth of the other. But it is well known that no man on earth lives up to his moral and spiritual ideal. The angel veils his face as he worships God; and the prophet cries, "Woe is unto me, for I am a man of unclean lips." No man has practised all he has inculcated, even in the most pious and concise writings. Dr Johnson points this well in a conversation in the Hebrides. "No man practises so well as he writes. I have all my life-long been lying till noon, yet I tell all young men, and tell them with great sincerity, that nobody who does not rise early will ever do any good. Only consider, you read a book, and are convinced by it, though you do not know the author; and suppose you afterwards know him and find that he does not practise what he teaches, are you to give up your former conviction? At this rate you would be kept in a state of uncertainty when reading every book till you knew how the author practised. There is something noble even in publishing truth though it condemns oneself."

What our young men of "Doubting Castle" want is more light and more charity. They and all others ought to try to distinguish between men who are thoroughly false and hypocritical, and those who are apparently inconsistent—to distinguish between both classes and the evidence and the validity of the creed they profess to believe. Looking at Christianity, and sometimes at God, through a distorted medium—the bad conduct of the *mere* professors of religion—how could he be happy? how could he have a proper view of God, and the means by which God proposes to save man? Impossible! And yet this was where our young friend erred, and where thousands have erred. And one mistake leads to others, and that which generally follows the one just named is having too much confidence in their own opinion. We say so without in any way reflecting on their abilities or earnestness. Indeed, young doubters of his class are always tremendously in earnest. As we have seen, soon after the great mistake of undervaluing Christianity, because some of those who said they were on its side did not act in the most desirable manner, comes that of adhering "through thick and thin" to notions formed when all the surrounding circumstances combined most unfavourably to prevent the views from being strictly correct, and, at that time, not expansive. His knowledge of real life and Bible truth was necessarily very incomplete, and opinions formed on half information cannot be always altogether sound. At the very time Mr Hillocks was being seriously injured in mind, he was in the thick of a fierce political battle—the agitation being at fever heat, red hot. How could he at that time calmly examine those things which make for our peace? Whatever was wrong, however injurious, and even dangerous to simple, earnest, religious life—such as the young man desired to see and feel—yet the inference he drew from what he saw and heard could not be always and altogether correct. We repeat, more light and more charity is much wanted by all, but especially by earnest young men.

We might close this chapter—convinced that none will be readier than Mr Hillocks to give us credit for the best of motives in speaking freely to young men on these points—but as they are important to all, we must yet speak of another common mistake into which he also fell. Never was he known to countenance any of the vices of the day. To such he gives no quarter; but, in his more juvenile writings, he presents a plea for those who did not wait on the means of grace, and which is worthy of notice here. For instance, he tells us that during his *first* visit to Luthermuir— about three months—he was not once in the Church, which was close by where he lodged, and then proceeds to defend himself and others. Though he deplored the heedlessness and the dissipation of many of his fellow-workmen—most of whom drank or lounged about all the Day of Rest, without meeting with God's people for worship—yet he seems to blame the worshipping people more than those who neglected to walk as God desires all. To his credit be it said, he does not bring forward the usual plea—the want of ability on the part of the ministers. There has been a succession of excellent ministers in Luthermuir, such as the late James Renwick, who was regarded as the Apostle of the district. The excuse was the want of Sunday clothes, and this excuse he thus rather keenly sustained :

"The over enthusiastic in religious matters may say, 'A poor excuse; could they not hear a sermon in rags as in rich apparel?' I answer, 'Yes, they could.' But why do *you* not go to church in your working clothes, when you see so many staying at home because they *cannot* dress like you? Before you accuse the poor unfortunates of false pride, lay your *own* pride aside and do what you can to reform the mental and social condition of the poor. If this cannot be done, leave your Sunday dress at home, and then those who have no other than their working clothes will come and sit beside you. Remember that the same spirit that induces you to put on your *best* to go to church makes those who have no *best* stay at home; and be assured that while you are feasting on the blessed truths of the Gospel, they must get something to satisfy their minds, and this may be good or bad, according to the company they are in. Do not forget that you are partly to blame for so many absenting themselves from the church. Send your missionaries to those poor benighted heathen round your own localities as well as to foreign lands. True charity begins at home, though it should not end there."

This is spirited and special pleading; but perhaps he forgot that the weavers would have had better clothes and felt more inclined to attend divine service had they worked on the Monday and Tuesday, instead of lounging or dissipating on these days, and, in many cases, drinking on Saturday afternoon and Sunday. It is well for all to look at both sides of these important questions; and this will no doubt be done by Mr Hillocks in the promised work to which we have already referred, and which, from the nature of the subject, must be interesting.

CHAPTER VIII.

THE TEACHER IN HIS FIRST SCHOOL.

HIS FIRST "SESSION."

RESUMING the narrative at the point we left, at the close of Chapter IV., we find the "Young Weaver" converted into a youthful "Dominie." And we are glad to add here that—to the joy of the parents of his charge, and the lasting benefit of those who were brought under his influence—"the second and brighter dawn" had burst into the clear day ere this event. He could say, "I thank God for the light and peace. That which I believed, because my parents or Sunday School teachers told me, I now believe because I have searched and examined for myself."

Let us see how he lived, and how he studied and succeeded in this his first public charge—

His first session, as teacher, was from the opening day till the usual "vacations" in 1845. He says, "The small bills announcing the opening of my school, simply held out that I was to teach reading, writing, and arithmetic. Latin and mathematics were not mentioned, because I knew but little of either—at least, I could not profess to teach them. Detesting such quackery as too often springs from the vanity of young men when becoming teachers, I preferred to follow the advice—

'Let all the foreign tongues alone,
Till you can read and spell your own.'"

He began with ten very young boys and girls—each paying the fee of twopence per week—one shilling and eightpence on which to live and pay expenses! Ultimately, however, his school began to increase slightly in this curious way. When any urchin in the neighbouring schools became, by habit and repute, a truant, he was sent to the "Laddie's School." The word "Laddie," the Scotch for boy, being used here because the teacher was short in stature, as well as young in years. His miniature seminary by-and-by became a minor cave of Adullam. At first, the "Laddie" is much perplexed by his little ragged regiment. In a short time, however, he gets into their way, and learns to manage and instruct them; and the "Cave" becomes the celebrity of the district. He displayed, even then, those uncommon powers for which he is so well-known, of winning the children to love and learning, even the youngest as well as the roughest. Still, for a considerable time, his assembly was very poor, and comparatively thin; and this put him to his wits' end to know how to live till the better time should come.

By this time, his father and family had also left Lochee and returned to Dundee, not far from his school-house. To the struggling teacher, this suggested the idea, and gave the opportunity of weaving late at night and early in the morning without anyone knowing of it save his own family. "For," says he, "strange to say, had the public known I was put to such shifts, I might have closed my school door." "But," he adds, "I had soon to give up weaving by stealth. Having but one suit of clothes, there was no possibility, even with all my brushing, of getting rid of the weaver's livery when going to school."

Playfully alluding to these and other difficulties—more especially during the first year or so of his life as a teacher—he says, "This effort having failed, another must be made. Only think of living within the means on less than five shillings a week! And yet it must be done. House-rent was out of the question. I found the school-house rent quite enough, therefore the humble seminary had to answer the purpose of cooking, dining, and *drawing* room. As for a servant, that was impossible, so I served myself. But where could I find the effectual disinfectant so as not to alarm the craving stomachs of my not over-fed charge, on their assembling with me 'after dinner'—how could the flavour of the roast beef and plum pudding be extinguished? I got over this difficulty by adopting the logician's maxim—remove the cause and the effect will cease. The fact is, I was, on uncontrovertible grounds, a vegetarian, and without the figs or grapes. Nor had I much difficulty in putting my cooking utensils out of sight—a small kettle, a little jug, and tin spoon, served my purpose.

"Here was the order of the day—day by day for a considerable time. I began my studies in the school-room early in the morning, and continued till nine. Then I had a 'plain breakfast,' after which I went out to have a little fresh air and a race with my pupils in the playground till ten o'clock, when the public *labours* of the day commenced. Between one and two, after the scholars went to dinner, I had my luncheon—a few peas or a little favourite gingerbread, with a little water. At five, after my scholars had gone for the day, I had 'a tea dinner'—that is, a cup of coffee and a biscuit. After reading till seven, I went to get private lessons in Latin, returned at nine, studied till eleven, then went to bed.

"The only variation from this course was when my enthusiasm made me forget myself, and remain longer at night than usual; and on Sunday when I went twice or thrice to church, and paid more special attention to religious subjects—collecting Bible facts and other Scriptural information for my pupils and my own enlightenment. From the first, I considered it was my duty to teach Christian precept as well as to impart general knowledge."

We give the following sentences as his experience:—

"Long before the School Board controversies," he says, "I

felt convinced that every teacher should be an enlightened Christian as well as an intelligent servant, but I never ventured to teach any special creed by way of explaining the Catechism; yet, to me, it was delightful to carry my charge through Scriptural biography, especially the life of Christ; and often did I read to them His sermon on the Mount and the twenty-third Psalm, and their pleasure seemed to increase with mine, all of us became so loving and so happy."

THE UNEXPECTED EXAMINATION.

From the commencement of the second session, comparative success was evident. He lived and laboured much as before, but by his great perseverance he overcame many difficulties, and gradually, though slowly, rose from beneath what at one time threatened to be a crushing pressure. In time, his comfort increased with his pupils; and ultimately the young teacher was recognised by his "brethren in the profession," and he was invited to become a member of the Forfar, Perth, and Fifeshire Teachers' Association. This honour he accepted, and continued to advance both in scholastic learning and social position.

From this time clergymen of note frequently visited his school, and every examination added new laurels to his brow. All united in commending his system of teaching and the proficiency of his pupils. We, too, were among those who enjoyed our visits to Smithfield Academy while under the care of Mr Hillocks. Referring to him elsewhere, we have said, and we here repeat—He that winneth children must himself be a child, partaking of many of the finer qualities which make childhood a thing so wonderful, so unique, and almost so divine. It is easy to terrify children, not difficult to cram them with knowledge; but to win them at once to yourself and to the love of learning is a rare and peculiar, although a simple seeming task. It was always truly delightful to see the "Young

Weaver" presiding in school, a child amongst children, *leading* them, even as Una led her milk-white lamb, by the unseen cord of love to the green pastures and still waters of knowledge, and by those ways of spiritual wisdom which are pleasantness and peace.

But what may be called his crowning success in relation to numbers, came by means of an unexpected examination of his school by a deputation from the Dundee Presbytery of the Church of Scotland. The messenger sent to express the desire of those appointed to visit and examine the school, called on Saturday evening, and said the deputation wished, if possible, to come on the Monday morning following. " This is as sudden as it is unexpected," said the teacher to himself ; but readily consented, on condition that the reason for coming without due notice be given to the parents and others who might come to the examination. The children assembled about ten o'clock, but were sent home at once, to tell their parents the news, with the strict injunction to be all in the play-ground a quarter before eleven o'clock. A few minutes after this, the words " They are coming," from the lips of some of the girls, called the teacher to welcome the visitors. " They were yet a little distant," he says, " but I found it difficult to keep from laughing right out. At the point where I saw them the path was narrow, so they had to walk one abreast. First came the good Minister of St Andrew's Church, the Rev. Mr Logan, who was lame; then followed his worthy man, who was also lame ; and the next was a fine faithful dog, also lame ; and behind all was a very tall, but, at that time, rather spare man, the Rev. John Tulloch, now the famed Principal Tulloch, of St Andrew's University.

" I was glad that some of my boys, inclined to be risible, did not observe this triple *hirple*, which, at first, so tickled me. Having suppressed the smile, I was able, in a becoming manner, to introduce the strangers to those of the parents who had been able to come, notwithstanding the short notice ; and seeing the two ministers and 'the man' seated—and the wise dog squatted quietly below his master's chair—I gave the signal for the scholars to enter and take their places.

"I told the deputation that I and my pupils were under their direction, and put into their hands a syllabus of the week's work. Mr Logan expressed a desire that I go on as usual with any branch of training he or Mr Tulloch might suggest; and then he very kindly told the parents present that the desire to see the school in its true and general working order was the only reason why they had come so suddenly after my consent. The examination went on for three hours, and glad was I to hear the hearty expression of approbation.

"This did me great good, and I was glad; so were the children and their parents. Thus encouraged, our enthusiasm increased with my popularity."

THREE IMPORTANT INCIDENTS.

After spending "the vacation" in Edinburgh, as before—becoming more proficient in what he had learned by private lessons in Dundee—he opened his "Third Session." Again his school filled, and he was once more at home with his happy and obedient charge. Having so completely won their affections that he obtained a complete rule (of kindness) over them that he could venture to try some very important experiments with them, they cheerfully and heartily seconded his every effort to give a pleasing variety in the more general as well as the ordinary instruction. One of these experiments may not, in one sense, be regarded as educational, and yet it is closely connected and worthy of the attention of teachers. According to the usual custom in schools this effort might have proved to be the most difficult of all; but in his case it was the easiest, though about the last of his many successes during his first three years as a public teacher. Under his care, and with their training, he had only to ask and it was done. He says, "I asked them (his pupils), if they would help me to govern without corporal punishment. Of course their ready answer was 'yes,' and they meant what they said. After explaining myself and reasoning with them, we resolved to try for a week, and succeeded. After that we tried for a month, and succeeded. And, seeing my way clear, we, in triumph, banished the *taws*—then the dread of every Scotch boy and girl."

Love was the conqueror, and with joyous triumph he inwardly said—

"I'm monarch of all I survey, my right there is none to dispute."

And this went on to the close of the session, which was rather earlier than was general in that district—he having again gone beyond his strength, and become so weak that immediate rest became imperative.

Here we may record three of the interesting incidents associated with these first three years of his life as a public teacher. They have been important to others as well as to those then more immediately concerned.

As has been said, Mr Hillocks deserves well of those interested in the Temperance cause, having been one of its most earnest and consistent supporters; but here is the first time we hear of his avowed adhesion to the Total Abstinence principles. He says—"Soon after I became popular as a teacher, I was favoured with invitations to spend the evenings. These invitations, though mostly coming from the parents of my pupils, I uniformly declined, being still anxious for my advancement; but, as a rule, I devoted an hour each evening, and, in time, visited all the parents and guardians of my charge.

"The parents of five children—two of whom were at my school—were among the first I visited in this way. After talking with the mother for some time, she looked to one of the elder girls. There was a meaning in that look. The girl went to the cupboard, took something from it, and placed that something under her apron. In a short time she returned, replacing the something—so I thought—and then began to prattle with the children as before. She seemed a little confused-like, as if she had done something that was not altogether right. When I was about to leave, the good woman said, 'Nae, nae, mester, ye maun taste wi's afore ye leave,' and took a small bottle from the cupboard, from which she filled a glass. As I stood, many thoughts rushed through my mind, all centring on the question 'Shall I accept or refuse?' The woman had an honest face; and, no doubt, a kind heart, and desired thus to manifest her respect towards me. But I saw something wrong. The money, however small, was spent on that which was worse than useless. And there was the slyness and the confusion of the girl. Out of respect to the good intentions of the mother, I put the glass to my lips, but did not suffer the liquid to touch my tongue. There and then I resolved, as this was the first time, so it would be the last time my lips would touch strong drink by way of the drinking customs. And, by the help of God, I have been able to keep my resolution—never to give, never to take any intoxicating liquors as a token of friendship or hospitality.

"Since then I have been enabled to form temperance societies and bands of hope not a few, using the Temperance Movement as an important handmaid to the Gospel."

This visiting convinced him more and more that it is well that the teacher knows as much as possible of the position and condition of the pupils and their parents. Referring to the second incident to which we refer, he says:—

"Though one may try, as I always tried, to show no respect of persons—neither in pupils nor parents—yet there are always a few who show a greater interest in you and to whom you can therefore speak with more freedom. Such was my experience.

For instance, there were not far from the school a happy pair. The husband sober and sensible; the wife clean and cheerful; with children to match—sweet, winning, intelligent. This mother spoke to me of many important matters, and one was the propriety of my settling down under a good pastor in some church instead of going a Sunday here and a Sunday there. I was easily persuaded, because my own mind had been running in the same line of thought. Of course, she recommended her own minister, with whom I was somewhat acquainted, and about whose manner there was something very pleasing and attractive. I soon felt there was also much in the pulpit of an attractive nature. The delivery was often masterly, the voice musical, the words choice, and the matter instructive. I became, and for some considerable time continued to be, a member of his church, to my profit as well as my pleasure. That minister was the Rev. J. R. (now Dr) McGavin of Tay Square United Presbyterian Church."

But this was not all that was gained. Friendships, and something even more endearing, were formed in the course of these cursory visits. This is seen in the third incident—perhaps the most important, to him at least—that which in its ultimate results ended in linking his destiny to that of his most excellent wife, introduced to the readers of "Life Story" by the pleasing title of "Auntie Maggie." He says, "Among my first pupils was a sweet girl named Aggie. Her father was not of the ordinary stamp of minds. He had read a good deal, and had elevated ideas of teaching, at least so far as intellectual facts, and the mode of teaching them, were concerned. He had often expressed a wish to meet me, and I was as anxious to have a conversation with him.

"When I called, there was present, on a visit, a favourite relative, from Edinburgh, called Auntie Maggie. But Auntie took very little part in the conversation. She *seemed* so taken up with her chattering niece, watching with quiet delight the varied movements of the endearing child, who frequently leaped upon my knee, and then looked into my face so bewitchingly that the stranger could not well comprehend how the child could be so free and affectionate, never having before seen scholar and teacher so happy.

"'Auntie Maggie,' said I to myself, after Aggie's father and I had done with the philosophical subjects. 'Auntie Maggie,' I added, almost audibly, for I could scarcely help myself; 'there is something so sweet in the name and lovely in its owner.' And suddenly I had to chide myself for having taken a sly peep into the loveliest face I have ever seen. But it was no use to check and chide myself, for, in a moment, I was *smitten*—that spark was kindled in my soul which the poets call love."

CHAPTER IX.

OTHER SCHOOLS AND OTHER SCHOLARS.

BOTANY CLASSES AND LITERARY SOCIETIES.

By the time the school was closed, he was so overpowered by hard work—learning and teaching—that he was scarcely able for his annual journey to Edinburgh, far less to apply himself, as he had previously done, to the use of such means as led to his advancement in Scholastic knowledge. But he was not disheartened; never was he at a loss. In him necessity was ever the mother of invention. Referring to this period, he says, "I had heard of what was called Lord Brougham's rule—'When he was tired walking, he rode; and when he was tired riding, he walked;' and this suggested to me that as I was not then able to follow in the path of the schoolmen, as I had previously done, I should think of another school, not less genial, but less severe on the mind—the field, with book in hand. This was a happy thought, bringing to my mind the fact that what is right can never be lost, *if rightly done.* When striving to encourage my scholars, I opened botanical as well as biographical classes. In the first I was greatly assisted by the knowledge and experience of one of our literary companions, Mr George (now Professor) Lawson. His kind and useful hints were given in letters, and in the first of which there was this sentence, 'I highly approve of your proposal to teach your young charge the rudiments of Natural History. It has long been my conviction that were the people more addicted to the study of such a pleasant subject they would be all the happier for it. It would greatly improve the moral feelings.' So far as my pupils were concerned, I found he was right. But the good thus begun accompanied me when I was no longer able to teach. By this time my love for flowers gave me additional delight in examining the various conformations and learning the valuable properties of plants. And this was the very thing that did me good, when, perhaps, I might have gone to bed instead; and then I was always improving a little, and I now turned my attention to medical botany.

"But I was enabled at this time to realise, in another direction, that nothing was lost. I loved my book as well as the field, and delighted to think of the benefit of the profitable nights spent in " The Halls of Lamb," in connection with the various literary societies that met there. Speaking from experience, I would say to every young man, however pressed for time and means in following out a given course of study, a night given, say weekly—cheerfully, heartily, and wisely—in a genial and generous literary society, is sure to be so much gain. Apart from the facilities it is likely to afford for mental culture and mutual improvement, it helps to brush away some of the fantastical notions from the minds of those who are apt to suffer from an abundance of pleasant fancies and whimsical ideas—such as vanish in the presence of sound knowledge. And more, a good society, well conducted, is also of great value to those who at first may be rather timid. I have known such to be very awkward to begin with, yet, in time, pick up a little of that courage which is always necessary in the defence of a good cause. Never had I reason to regret the acquaintanceship formed at that time with those of a literary turn of mind; and, to this day, I rejoice in the lasting friendship of genial souls. I am the more grateful to such, because I was then so far behind them—they having previously given themselves up to the study of literature. When

I was first introduced to them I had read little save books on the art of teaching, and such as had a tendency to advance me in my profession as a teacher. This deficiency on my part led me to bear a low sail, so that, for a time, I was little other than a silent partner. Ultimately, however, they urged me on and pushed me forward till I ventured to read an essay occasionally. Then it was that *they* had their enjoyment. If I had been inclined to be uncharitable, I might have supposed that they had induced me to come thus far forward to become a target for their sharp-shooting, which they called 'fair criticism.' Of course I was all the better for the 'sharpening up.' It drew me out in self-defence, and latterly I took a share in the regular debates, many of which seemed to be as hot as a set battle."

HIS LITERARY ASSOCIATES.

To win a prize, Mr Hillocks was induced to speak of himself; but he has also spoken of others, and that in hearty praise. This we find in connection with his first literary associates. He says, "When I think of the lives and efforts of many of those with whom I met in the various literary societies, their experience confirms my own—that mental culture in youth is of great service in active business and general usefulness. Some of these earlier friends have passed away, but not without leaving a few 'footprints on the sands of time.' First of all was one of my latest tutors, before I became a public teacher, the late Rev. George Hunter, afterwards the able and respected minister of the United Presbyterian Church, Tillicoultry. He introduced me in the way of obtaining the benefits in which I now rejoice.

"There, too, was Robert Leighton, the poet, the author of 'The Whittle.' He died in Liverpool at the early age of 47, but not before he gave marked proofs of the earlier promise seen in his intense thoughtfulness. It has been said, 'What Burns did for the plough, Robert Leighton did for the counting-house.'

"And then there was James Adie, who devoted himself to the study of Geology. Being very modest, loving, and gentle, he became the favourite of all who knew him and understood him. Because of this, and being passionately fond of poetry, especially Hogg's beautiful Idyl, he was called 'the Gentle Kilmany.' He went to Canada and became connected with the press there, where he was known as a dutiful son, a faithful husband, a loving father, an enthusiastic student, a useful man. But, when returning from a jury trial, he was overtaken by a snow-storm, and afterwards found dead in the neighbourhood of Niagara—a sad event, which created profound sorrow throughout the country.

"And of those who have manifested that enlightened zeal which was at that time fostered in Dundee—and who are still active in their own special walks of life—is Professor Lawson, the kindly and manly friend already mentioned as having assisted me in the study of the interesting science in which he shines. George Lawson was not unlike 'the Gentle Kilmany' in winning ways, but he seemed to me to take a firmer grip of his theme—Botany. He began life as a lawyer's clerk, but he began early to devote his mornings to rambles in the neighbourhood of Dundee, and continued thus to botanize till he knew every plant and flower there within a radius of seven miles. He also studied hard with the view of preparing himself for a situation more in harmony with his tastes—contributing to magazines and newspapers. This attracted the attention of the Edinburgh Scientific Institution, and he became Secretary to the Edinburgh University, and latterly became assistant to Balfour, Professor of Botany. In the first he was succeeded by Alexander Smith, the poet; and in the second by John Saddler, the botanist. He is now the very able and highly-esteemed Professor of Chemistry of Dalhousie College, Halifax, Nova Scotia.

"And there are others still at home, or at least not far distant from the scene of their first literary efforts. Nearly allied in the course of study is Councillor William Ogilvie, Banker, Lochee, a keen botanist, and the superintendent of a thriving Children's Church. There, too, is the kindly-hearted William Stiven, the prosperous accountant, who was better known for the papers he read than the speeches he made. John L. Cunningham, still noted for his tact, zeal, and activity. John Sime, a teacher in the quiet village of Lantrathen, but better known as the writer of some excellent parodies, such as 'The Halls of Lamb,' after Byron's 'Isles of Greece.' The Rev. John Hunter, Congregational Minister, Aberdeen, who wrote some poems on rural life, and whose Special Discourses on the Revelation attracted considerable attention. Isaac Peterkin, the Alyth Orator, whose style is elaborate, yet fresh, free, and full of life, having in his time drawn largely from Pitt and Fox, Brougham and Johnson, Bacon and Blair. His favour is courted for his hearty geniality as well as his social position and undoubted influence. Charles C. Maxwell, the successful merchant, and who, because of his fine taste and happy humour, is still the favourite of literary circles. Occasionally he lectures on such subjects as 'Waterloo,' 'Thomas Hood,' and 'The Scotch Language.' He is a lover of rare books, especially those printed in Dundee; and his selection of valuable pictures, as well as his store of ancient curiosities, show that they have been collected together for their beauty. But what is better still, is the pleasing fact that not a little of this special talent is now being concentrated in connection with a Mission Meeting in one of the lowest places of Dundee.

"From all this it may well be inferred that a literary taste, when well directed, may greatly assist in the rising of that tide which may run on either to fortune or usefulness, sometimes to both. Many others might be named, but I shall only mention other two—men of quite another stamp, but no less representative, showing the benefit of mental culture in early life. I couple them here, because in those days they were always together—one is Peter Begg, now connected with the *Dundee Advertiser*. From the first he was known as a great reader and a keen debater, but that which revealed his special power in this way was a series of letters which appeared in the *Dundee Advertiser* in relation to a strike which was then attracting considerable attention in the town. The ability and the style of the writer were noticed by Mr Leng, the able editor of that newspaper, ending in an appointment at once congenial and useful. But that upon which Mr Begg looks with triumphant joy, as the most important event in his life, was the part he took in the establishing of the Dundee Free Public Library. It is said, to him chiefly Dundee owes the benefits she now enjoys through the successful working of this much appreciated institution. And I know he has been very helpful in assisting other towns to participate in like privileges.

"The other member of the first literary society which I joined was James Scrymgeour. Indeed he was the first one with whom I formed anything like friendship; and in this we were one, though not always one in opinion. In our meetings we were often at counterpoints. We fought, with words of course, like two lawyers in a court of justice; but, like them, too, we shook hands after the battle was over. He was well advanced when I was a mere beginner, and this gave him the power, which he seemed to enjoy, of coming down upon me— as he said, '*of levelling hillocks.*' But though on such occasions he seemed to be rather strong, hasty, and fiery, there was always something that kept us united. Since then his field of labour has been so wide, and his efforts have been so many, that it is difficult to say for what he is best known, unless it is in being abler to help others than he has been to help himself; and in this sense, at least, we are yet one. 'I am a puzzle to myself, a perfect riddle.' So he said lately, by way of a reply to a question I put to him as to his *leading forte*, that in which he felt most congenial. Though he is very useful in connection with 'the Prisoners' Aid Society,' a local preacher among the Wesleyan Methodists, a public speaker in connection with Bands of Hope, temperance, and other societies, he also frequently gives evidence that he has the pen of a ready writer, especially when anything in the way of Natural History has to be done. He has also written a few brief memoirs, his special effort in that way being a tenderly-written notice of the Hon. and amiable Mrs Reginald Ogilvie, the only daughter of Lord and Lady Kinnaird."

BENEFIT OF MENTAL CULTURE.

There is enough here to convince all interested in the safety and usefulness of young men, that practically, as well as theoretically, it is well to encourage them in their mental as well as their spiritual improvement. There cannot be a grander aim, a nobler work, than the directing of every possible effort, so as to bring before our young men the Gospel in all its fulness, that they may desire to be, and really become, true disciples of the Lord Jesus Christ, in doctrine and life. But the mark will be greatly missed if, in connection with this, mental culture be disregarded. Reason is essential to the proper direction of one and all of the moral elements of our being; and the power of reasoning is never found where the culture of the intellect has been neglected. As the eye to the physical form, so is the intellect to the propensity—without the former the latter is blind. This groping in the dark is always dangerous, and in our day it is sinful, as well as painful. The atrocities of paganism and the intolerance of sectarianism owe much of their bigotry and venom to this blindness, to the absence of a cultivated intellect.

Impressions such as these must have suggested the following sentences to Mr Hillocks, in his lecture on "Mental Culture." He says, "I entreat every young man to seek *first* the Kingdom of God and His righteousness; but be sure also to see to the culture of the mind. There is an important truth in Christ's words, 'Without Me ye can do nothing.' It is from this standpoint I see the wisdom as well as the love in His urgent request—'Abide in Me, and I in you." Man, without the life and love of God in his soul, is weak and wretched. Whatever his other possessions, whatever his other attainments, mere intellect without true morality, is despicable and dangerous. Mental energy without spiritual power cannot promote the greatest good. Union with God, through Christ by the Spirit, is the source and centre of immediate and lasting usefulness. But great and grand and essential as our moral and spiritual susceptibilities are; grateful to God as we ought ever to be for all the gifts and graces which He has so graciously and so lovingly given—and which, when sanctified, give dignity and glory to our life and effort—yet we must not forget the duty and benefit of intellectual culture. This is necessary in every department and degree of improvement, personal and relative. It is indispensable to the proper and profitable study of nature and religion, to the attainment and enjoyment of all that our heavenly Father has laid before us touching belief and practice, health and happiness, the life here and the life hereafter.

"The truth is, when I think of the results of the efforts made in mental culture in the Dundee Literary Societies, I am reminded of the fact that there are other schools than the merely scholastic, and other scholars than those who are favoured with the stated curriculum of our regular colleges. Let us have all, if possible; if not all, all we can. I do not wish to convey the idea that all who have turned their attention to mental culture and classical literature have realised all the pleasure that such a study is capable of affording—far less the profits of which we hear so much—still, the most of us, in our own small way, have, in a measure, felt what Coleridge has said, that poetry was to him 'Its own exceeding great reward,' and that is something. It is a great gain, and is generally obtained by those who, from Christian motives and for holy aims, have had that hungering after profitable knowledge and the thirsting for celestial wisdom which are generally connected with the cultivation of the mind—especially where mutual improvement is associated with spiritual progress. I know there are exceptions to this general rule, but these generally follow when God and goodness have been forgotten. As the private student and the public teacher, I gave the Literary Society its place, *regarding it more as a means of recreation than instruction.*"

The italics are ours, and we call special attention to them, because they show that our friend has here fallen into the too common mistake. Whatever else he remembers, he never forgets a kindness done to him, whether by an equal or a superior. This is evident, not only in what he has just stated in regard to Mr Thomas Lamb, but also in all he has said in connection with his associates; but he is not so true to the societies which were so useful to him. In these ten words he almost upsets, at least he greatly weakens, what he has otherwise so truly said. The truth is, in his experience—as is generally the case in such well-regulated societies—there *was* "*instruction*" as well as recreation—more of the first than the second. There might have been a few exceptions, but from what we can gather from Mr Hillocks' own account, almost all were more or less earnestly bent on "mutual improvement"—none more so than he was—and hence the benefit he gained has been with him wherever he has gone, assisting him in all he has done.

The "weekly night" in "The Halls of Lamb" was not mere child's-play, and he was so deeply interested in these training schools that he took an active part in more than one of them. In page 344 of that interesting volume, entitled "Dundee Celebrities of the Nineteenth Century," are these words :—"The Literary Emporium brought with it the now well-known and successful labourer among the poor in London—the Rev. James Inches Hillocks." This is true, but we learn that he was also a member of "The Dundee Temperance Mutual Improvement Society." It was in the "Emporium" he read his first "Essay on Liberty;" and it was in connection with the "Mutual Improvement" that he delivered his first Temperance Lecture—for one of the objects of this society was to help its members to become Temperance Advocates.

Surely this was more than "recreation." Both of the subjects were such as to demand and receive from him much thought and careful preparation. He knew that they would be severely criticised—even his manner as well as the matter—and then the themes were dear to him. Only think of the young, abstemious (though then a retired) Radical, with etymology on the brain, and the dictionary at his finger ends, master of the synonymes and overflowing with adjectives, preparing his first Essay on Liberty and his first Lecture on Temperance. This was not a mere pastime, and we know these were not his only efforts in that direction. To regard literary societies "more as a means of recreation than instruction," is to make a great mistake. Those who do so, and act accordingly, will never secure the benefit which generally surrounds these valuable institutions. Mr Hillocks did not do so, though the words to which we have taken exception seem to convey the idea. His closing words on this point are—"The Literary Society has been to me a most valuable school."

CHAPTER X.

SUDDEN CHANGES.

THE CHARGE OF BEING IMPRUDENT.

THE surprises in this chapter and other portions of his life have laid him open to the charge of being "somewhat imprudent" in matters which, if otherwise managed, might have led to increased and longer continued prosperity—at least from a financial point. This has been frequently suggested to him, but never more pointedly and kindly put than in a very appreciative letter written to him by one of the greatest statesmen and ablest writers of the day. After receiving answers to the several questions carefully put—clearing off a kind of mist which hung about some of the important incidents merely referred to in "Life Story"—this painstaking correspondent was pleased to express his satisfaction not only in words, but also by "a mark of his appreciation" of "Mr Hillocks' evident self-denial."

And something of the same kind must have entered the mind of Her Majesty the Queen, who, after reading the same book, commanded that some inquiries be made respecting the author. By Her Majesty's letter to him—written by C. B. Phipps, and dated Windsor Castle, November 23, 1860—we learn that these inquiries proved perfectly satisfactory, and that the Queen was pleased to forward a cheque *as a mark of her Majesty's appreciation.*

But all this troubled as well as cheered Mr Hillocks, so

much so that he referred to it in his note to the second edition of that book. In his *revised* copy of that note, he says, "As to the charge—if charge it be—of not being sufficiently explicit in relation to some of the very important incidents in the volume, I must make this confession: I have told the truth, and nothing but the truth, in regard to myself, but not the *whole truth in regard to those who injured me*, intentionally or unintentionally. My only excuse is this: I had no wish to heap upon them more punishment than their own conscience may inflict. And, since then, another reason has had a considerable force with me, namely, to give names and speak in detail would be to lessen the usefulness of those concerned in proportion to the influence of the book, which is now somewhat extensive. Rather than do this, I prefer to run the risk of being regarded as at times somewhat imprudent, knowing that truth shall triumph, and right shall reign."

IN A COUNTRY SCHOOL.

Yet true as all this is, it must be admitted that the sudden changes are at times "unaccountable" to those who may not have known the pressing nature of the impelling circumstances, together with the strong motives which generally suggested the step taken—that more being supposed by him as likely to lead to another "step nearer the mark." With him everything—even the noble profession of teaching the young, which, to him, was really a delightful task—seemed to be made subordinate to this thought: that of becoming an intelligent and faithful minister of the Gospel. This was uppermost in all his efforts, even when adverse circumstances seemed to utter the dreaded words, "This is impossible."

It was this thought, and the hope of realising it, that induced him to leave Edinburgh, after a few weeks of comparative rest, again to meet his affectionate and waiting charge at Smithfield Academy. The meeting was a joyous one, but not of long duration. It was soon evident that he was not able to sustain the responsibilities of his increasing school, especially as the only space he could command was not equal to the number that sought admission. By the Doctor's advice, seconded by many of his best friends, he reluctantly accepted of a small school in the country. This, as might be expected, was the cause of deep sorrow to the scholars and their parents. The parting scene was very touching. Even parents wept with their children, especially when they saw the younger portion of the scholars cling to him, as if they had resolved to keep him by force. He endeavoured to restrain his own emotion, but this served only to intensify his grief, the depth of which may be partially gathered from the following closing paragraph of a letter which he sent to them, to be read by his successor—"When I think of our past joys and our affectionate farewell—how you loved me so fervently, and clung to me so closely—my heart fills and the tears run. So identified have been my life and feelings with yours that you are yet the subject of my daily thoughts and nightly dreams. Your presence was never annoying to me, and mine was always welcomed by you. In all our trials and triumphs we sympathised and rejoiced with each other. And now, though we are separated for a time, we can pray for each other, and God will answer. He is everywhere present. He can and He will be with you in Dundee, and with me here with my new pupils. Even though we may not meet again, as teacher and scholars, we may all meet in heaven, as the sons and daughters of our Father in Christ. That God may guide and bless us, and all connected with us, is the earnest prayer of your former and ever affectionate teacher."

Nothing could be more favourable to his recovery than the change. Anxious to regain his strength as soon as possible, he read very little and studied less. This—and a desire to be as much as possible in the fields—gave him an opportunity of becoming acquainted with the district in which his lot was cast. Roundy Hill was the name of the locality in which the school was placed—a small hamlet situated at the meeting points of the parishes of Airlie, Glammis, and Kerriemuir. And, not a great way off, were Glammis Castle, casting its shadow of a thousand years upon the grand trees and princely policy around; the Reekly Linn thundering in its solitude, amidst crags and woods; and the "Bonnie house o' Airlie" standing in the centre of one of the most romantic regions of all Scotland. Here, too, he also became very successful as a teacher. He was not long at Roundy Hill School before the sons and daughters of the neighbouring farmers and others left the more distant schools to join those who had been with him from the commencement. And being a "considerable way ahead of the farthest advanced" of his pupils, teaching to him was as easy as it was delightful.

The reason of this success is incidentally given—as before, his power was love. He says, "It was during my first months at Roundy Hill, my second school, that I realised—perhaps more fully than before—how much I had been bound up with my former and first charge, knit in the sweet bonds of affection. Wherever I went—surrounded by the sublime or the beautiful—their lovely faces, sweet voices, and winning ways followed me. But, in course of time—and not very long either—I found there were other loving and lovable children, *scholars whom I could love and whose affections I could win.*"

BECOMES A CHEMIST'S APPRENTICE.

All this is delightful. Childhood led by affection is sweet; and by his freely mingling with the people he had become a general favourite, happy and genial in the healthy atmosphere of this plain and pleasant life. Realising the benefits of this recreation, he had become the very opposite of the Smithfield recluse, and no tea nor supper party was considered complete without "the teacher." And yet he became a chemist's apprentice!

Here we have one of those "unaccountable movements" to which we have lately referred. His leaving a prosperous town school for a school in the country, then in a very bad condition, was a matter of necessity; but to leave what had become "a paying concern," and all the healthy pleasure associated with it, for the drudgery which generally falls to the lot of an apprentice, certainly calls for explanation. But that is soon found in his having an "eye to business," *his* business being "advancement in knowledge, with the view of becoming more useful." He had gone to the country to regain health, and that was accomplished. He was thankful, but he could not longer "bear the idea of being half idle," and therefore he "made another effort to learn something *more.*"

It will also be remembered that in Lochee Dr Hood gave him instruction in chemistry, and so awakened in him a desire to renew that study as early as possible. "Now was the time," he said to himself, after having several conversations with the late Robert Grant, then the only chemist and druggist in Kerriemuir. "The arrangements," he adds, "were these: that I reside in Kerriemuir, in order to open and clean the shop in the mornings, and be otherwise useful, till Mr Grant arrived at nine o'clock; and that I return to the shop at five in the afternoon, remaining till ten in the evening, compounding and dispensing medicines. This gave me between nine and ten o'clock to dress, take breakfast, and walk to my school—a distance of about two miles; and from four to five to retrace my steps, and take tea. The only time I had for my three R's—reading, reflection, and recreation—being before seven in the morning, and after ten in the evening, but the last R was made up by the daily four mile walk from Kerriemuir to Roundy Hill and back."

This constant strain on body and mind must have been very severe to the teacher-druggist, and we suspect that during some of these evenings, even sometimes in the mornings, when most exhausted, he must have sighed for the Lochee or Luthermuir Loom. But he persevered, and for more than a year he continued thus to labour and to learn. Finding his strength giving way under the weight of the twofold calling, he felt it was his duty to resign the duties of the teacher for a time, and so apply his whole time to the study, preparation, and dispensing of medicine—filling his note-book and his mind with all the knowledge he could gather till the time of the engagement was completed, when Mr Grant declared he had found in his apprentice an able and honest, a diligent and faithful assistant."

THE DISAPPOINTED STUDENT.

Though for a time he only had the wages of an apprentice, yet the balance of his savings at Roundy Hill was such as enabled him to think of carrying out his intention of becoming a student at the Castle Hill Normal Institution, Edinburgh. But here he was somewhat disappointed in his object—to learn how he might become still more proficient in the art of teaching. He says:—

"Of Greek, Latin and Mathematics there were plenty. We heard the words *phileo* and *amo* often enough; but of love there was no sign. I was often led to think that the sentence, '*I love* the cane, and *delight* to use it,' should have been selected as the chief of the exercises in parsing. I pitied the poor trembling children who came to be *taught* by 'the students.' There were some exceptions—more especially on the part of the young lady students; but, as a rule, in this *Normal* Institution a kind word from a loving heart was a rare thing. And yet these men and women were being daily sent to different parts of the country as fit and proper persons to *care* for our children, to '*teach* the young idea how to shoot'—rather how to shout under the pain caused by the free use of the cane—cutting up the feelings as well as the flesh—daily consuming that high and holy principle, in which every teacher and pupil should participate—hourly calling forth all that is evil and perverse, and ruinous to all concerned, especially our children. Hence it is that much of our teaching is very little above the eagerly absorbed lessons taught in our streets by that ever active and always demoralising teacher, called 'Punch and Judy'—mutual hatred, constant fighting, and all the ills that follow from the time they meet till the hour they part.

"The education question is now more frequently before the public, and many are giving attention to what they call 'elementary education;' but my experience as a student and a teacher, leads me to say, the first element in all education is love. We may have learning, and learning is essential; we may give money, and money is necessary; but without mutual love, on the part of teacher and pupil, all is vanity and vexation of spirit. They must be as dear to each other as they are near to each other. They cannot get on rightly without love—a love that is tender, because it is true—a love that wins and grows—a love that refines, and makes us one in heart and in aim, anxious to promote the beneficent results that follow the preparation of our youth for the life that is, and the life to come.

"This," he continues "was what I desired, but I could not see much in this institution that was calculated to bring it about; and being a Dissenter—a member of a denomination which did not see the propriety of denominational schools—I felt greatly at a loss to know what to do. To leave one church for another, merely to obtain a school—even with the chance of testing what I conceived to be a better mode of teaching—I could not. I thought the arrangements pressed severely and unjustly; so I prayed most earnestly that the time might come when no special sect would have the monopoly in our educational management.

"But even here it was not all loss. Otherwise I took a lively interest in the institution, gathering from every possible source all the knowledge I could obtain as long as I remained—that was as long as my Kerriemuir savings lasted. And here, too, I wrote and published my first tractate, entitled 'The New Writer.'"

BECOMES TEACHER AND DRUGGIST AGAIN.

Having paid his way for his board and education at the Edinburgh Normal Institution, his means became so very limited that he had not much time in which to consider what the next step should be. He naturally thought of his native town and his promise to visit his former pupils as soon as possible. He was soon in the midst of his friends, who were glad to hear that he might be retained. Being invited to the old locality, in a few weeks he was surrounded by many of his former pupils as happy and affectionate as ever.

In six months the school-rooms were found to be too small, and larger premises were obtained; but in less than six months after there was overcrowding as before. As far as the scholars were concerned—in number, conduct, and progress—he was very successful; but that success, associated as it was with other causes, led him to resign. Larger premises could not be found in the locality at that time; he could not take in all who wished to come; and "bad times set in," so that the fees did not come up to enable him to meet the various claims demanding his immediate attention—not only his own support, but helping others whom he desired to assist, especially his dear father, who, by this time, was almost entirely laid aside. All this—and finding his own health again giving way under trying labours in a crowded school, without an assistant —made him think of another plan by which he might gain his object; and remembering that now he had two strings to his bow, he thought of taking advantage of his experience as a chemist and druggist. But this was connected with a difficulty not easily overcome. He says: "The thought of the amount of money necessary to start a business, made me at first think of becoming an assistant to some firm in that line. But then I thought if I had a shop I might so succeed as to be able to add to the stock by degrees. And in that case I might be able to give my father some light work *to please him*, for he could not bear to be idle when able to move, and he liked to do something for what he got from anyone, even from me. My sister, too, was in want of a situation, so I thought of her as my housekeeper—the place she held before I left Dundee for the country.

"Thus I built my castle, consisting of a house and shop, with my father, sister, and, at last, an assistant. 'It was a risk,' said a friend to me, some time after. And he was right, for my means were so small that I had to stock the shop little by little, after making ends meet. A business does not grow in a day. I made use of the other string of my bow. Though I gave up my public school, I continued to teach, going out as a tutor, and teaching private classes in my own house. In the former case, my father was present to say when I might be seen; and, in the latter, I was at hand should I be wanted."

There is something quite edifying in all this. Apart from the noble object, the tact and perseverance, there is something quaint in this combination—of teaching syllables and selling salts—distributing doses of castor oil and laying down the rules of composition. But though he "had not much with which to start business," he succeeded even beyond his expectation.

A CROWNING EVENT.

Here, in the Hilltown, he continued to push on in business till he heard of what was considered a better opening—a larger shop and much nearer the centre of the town. He removed, and again did well, taking an active part in all such efforts as he considered likely to promote the social and spiritual welfare of the people. It was while in this shop that he brought out the little book entitled, "Passages in the Life of a Young Weaver." It was "this humble production that awoke in us much of that hearty sympathy and kindly feeling" of which he has spoken in grateful terms. As was said at the time, "Few could read it without tears and smiles, and none without profit."

But the crowning event in this shop is yet to be told. Here his pen was often employed in writing other "Passages," also full of life and earnest thought. They were short and evidently to the point. In short, "Auntie Maggie" had come from Edinburgh to live with her parents, who had retired from the bustle of town life to a quiet neat cottage in Lochee. "They had," he says, "some beautiful flowers in their garden, and I went for my morning bouquet. Many a beauty I got, but none so beautiful as the fair one by whose hand each flower was gathered and given. For years the conviction that her worth was equal to her beauty had grown stronger in me, till it became too strong for the thought I had once entertained, not to marry till I had *finished* my education, as the phrase goes. At last—after a little more of the usual thinking about it—she said, 'Yes.'"

The result was, we had the pleasure in November, 1851, of linking their destinies in happy wedlock.

That this attachment was mutual and fortunate, that "the beauteous maiden" was made for our struggling hero, we have only to call as witness his own words—written not in the fervour of anticipation, but *after* the bliss of realisation—after she had proved herself to be, as he says, "one of the best of wives, and one of the most loving of mothers."

"We have had," he says, "reverses as well as successes. From causes over which we had no control, distress and poverty soon came upon us with all their deadly weight, sickening and sinking influences. More than once misfortune's blast swept away all we had, save love and hope; but this only proved the more her affectionate fidelity, tender solicitude, and undaunted heroism. Our great suffering—which I cannot here indicate, far less describe—tested those principles and manifested those feelings which adorn virtuous womanhood and bless those under its hallowed influence. The fiery furnace was often very hot, but we were one, and God was with us, hence we were not consumed. And, in the midst of our most trying hours, we were enabled to be helpful to those in want of help, realizing that usefulness in the work of the Lord is a blessed source of undying happiness.'

CHAPTER XI.

FROM DUNDEE AND BACK.

AN UNLOOKED FOR REWARD.

THE first of their reverses was not long in coming upon them. After their marriage they opened a new business in the drug line in Broughty Ferry—a bathing-place about four miles east of Dundee. At the beginning, and for some time after, they seemed bound to prosper. The happy pair, with their affectionate niece, Aggie, were much beloved by all who made their acquaintance, especially the poor. And yet a large portion of the time spent there—though far from being an entire blank—is deeply tinged with melancholy reflection. They suffered severely, and one of the causes was, they would not swerve from that rectitude which stamps the life of the upright—their "being true as well as faithful to the erring."

In these last nine words there is the essence of much that might be valuable to the novelist and exciting to the reader; but we prefer to pass on to one of those happy incidents on which Mr Hillocks loves to dwell. From the first they tried to be useful, and it was not long before they saw that the power of strong drink was too much for many here; and hence to try to meet the increasing evil results, they took the lead in the re-organisation of the Total Abstinence Society, and succeeded. But this is not the effort to which we refer as bringing "the unlooked for reward." Among their first efforts to help others was gratis teaching. Mr Hillocks says:—" Of those who were the first to come for medicine was a young man called Robert. He was a shoemaker's apprentice, and had suffered much pain in the chest ever since he had taken to the awl. It was clear his trade was against him, and I told him so. He could read and write but badly, and he knew nothing of casting accounts. This he told me in confidence, seeing I felt for him. I offered to help him. In time he soon improved so that he was able take a porter's situation, which was much more favourable to his health than any medicine I could give him.

"Years after, I was benighted in the country, in the midst of a great storm. The thunder roared, the lightning flashed, the rain fell in torrents, and the roads seemed to be one sheet of water. Having emerged from between the two woods which had been named to me as a guide to the first steps toward the village to which I was bound, a rise on the road enabled me to see the cross roads. But there I stood, not knowing which way to go. I saw a light in the distance, and thinking it was a light in some window for me, my first impulse was to make for it; but, on second thoughts, and while praying for guidance, I stood still. At last it appeared as if drawing nearer to where I was; and perceiving distinctly, I asked myself, who may these be? Are they likely to help or destroy? Hearing the sound of voices in conversation, I spoke, asking my way, even before I could well see who were approaching.

"'I can tell you the way, Mr Hillocks, but you cannot go there to-night,' said one of the two men.

"I thought I knew the voice, but could not remember the name of the speaker. It proved to be no other than Robert, who now held a responsible appointment at the very railway station I had lately left. He and another servant were on their way home to a hamlet not far from where I had been waiting.

"'You'll have my best room, a good supper, and a better breakfast, my friend,' said Robert, as he shook my hand most heartily, and then told his companion how and where we first met, and how God had blessed to him the lessons and kindness he received at Broughty Ferry.

"All this and more of the same kind he repeated to his tidy wife who had been anxiously waiting his return—all the more anxious because of the dreadful thunder-storm which yet raged. I do not know for which I was most thankful to God —the welcome shelter, or the sympathising heart which led us to help Robert to open this door of refuge in the night of trouble.

"'With God, nothing is lost,' said I to myself, as I retired to rest that night, weeping for joy—a joy in which my beloved help-meet shared as I next day related the incident to her."

AT GAULSWELL SCHOOL.

Our friends wisely resolve to leave Broughty Ferry, the scene of their first sorrows. He accepted a very timely invitation to become the teacher of Gaulswell school, connected with Banff estate, near Alyth, and then under the kindly patronage of the late Sir James Ramsay. This happy change was a great improvement. The teacher was once more restored to his proper element, and his devoted partner in life manifested her readiness to assist him in his duties in making the best of their altered circumstances. But it was some time before they could forget the ills through which they had passed. This is evident in a letter written some time after to their friend, the late Alexander Laing, the author of "Wayside Flowers." After detailing the distressing causes and the penniless condition into which they had been suddenly thrown, Mr Hillocks says: "Even yet the agony and anguish of the past make me shudder. Words cannot describe the dark shades of grief and sadness caused by our sudden transition from prosperity to adversity. We are still suffering from its direful effects, but we are thankful to God and happy in each other. The country air and kindly feeling which we so much enjoy at our new home will, no doubt, soon restore us to health and strength, giving back our former natural cheerfulness and helping us to laugh to scorn the ills of life."

The school-house was small, but the garden was large. The income was not much, but the wants were few, and those who were able were kind, glad to see their children so happy, and anxious to have their "lessons all right."

A Sunday-school was also opened, and well encouraged, some coming from a long distance. "A mutual loan library," was also established, and popular lectures were occasionally given. And in all this Sir James took an active interest, speaking highly of the teacher, while increasing his facilities to usefulness. The late Professor Ramsay also called and congratulated all concerned—not forgetting Mrs Hillocks' "little palace," nor the jug at the well, placed there by her that the wayfarer might drink of the pure spring and be refreshed.

Here, in the "little palace," a boy was born, and was named after the editor of these chapters. But the joy that such an event was almost certain to cause became soon overshadowed by sorrowful intelligence from Dundee, summoning them there to witness the approaching death of Mr Hillocks' father. The Sailor-weaver had something to say to his son and daughter. He was also anxious to see their baby-boy before he left "this vale of tears."

"I am happy in Jesus," said the old tar, anxious to console the weeping ones now gathered around him.

"That is right and joyous, father," said the son, gently patting the cold cheek of his dying sire, aged by poverty more than by years.

"Yes, yes," said the young mother, still weak, but anxious

to do her duty to one who loved her. "There, now, father, that's much better," she added, having smoothed the pillow and laid the aching head gently down.

"All right, I'll soon be aloft. I am happy. God bless you both, and your dear boy. May he be as great a blessing to you as you have been to me."

The old man would have said more, but he and all around were overcome. He died in a few days after this interview. Our friend adds: "We were thankful I was able to do a son's part to a suffering father—suffering from honest poverty, for his was never self-inflicted. I thought—and there was something akin to bitterness in the thought—how such as my poor father, who had fought our nation's battles and won our national victories were left to starve, while others who did no more, perhaps not so much, knew not how to waste the wealth thrust upon them. But then the gall in this strain of thought was partly extracted by the remembrance of the efforts which my father made to give me a few weeks' schooling, and how that God in His providence so blessed that effort that it became the means of helping me to gratify his last wish on earth."

BACK TO HIS OLD HAUNT.

His special efforts on the Banff Estate attracted the attention of some of the correspondents to the neighbouring newspapers. This, in turn, called the attention of committees and others interested in schools to Mr Hillocks, leading to a correspondence, and latterly to an engagement on his part to become the teacher of another school. Perhaps this was an error, but it was done for the best. His aspiration formed motives which were ever commendable, but the steps which they urged were not always wise—looking at the matter from a merely money-making point of view. In this case, he thought he was so much stronger that he could carry on a larger school, which was likely to give him a larger income, and so help him on once more to Edinburgh, the seat of the learning he desired.

When leaving, Sir James gave Mr Hillocks an additional token of his kindness; also a letter in which he was pleased to state that he had every reason to be satisfied with him as an able and successful teacher; that the ministers and others who attended the examination of the school, when under his charge, entertained a high opinion of his qualifications and general character; and the *Dundee Advertiser* took the lead in the press in recounting in pleasant terms the various efforts he had made for the educational and general good at Gaulswell school.

The minister who corresponded with Mr Hillocks, in connection with the new school, addressed his letter, Muirton Laurance Kirk, and for this spot the teacher, the young mother, and their first born, started early one morning—arriving as directed, at Mary Kirk Station, on the Dundee and Aberdeen Railway. At first he was troubled, because Laurance Kirk Station had not been given, but passed the matter from his mind, believing that the station given might be nearer to "Muirton." And so it was.

One of the members of the School Committee was waiting at the station to conduct them to their new home. But imagine Mr Hillocks' surprise when he found that Muirton Laurance Kirk was no other than a part of Luthermuir, his old haunt; that he had, by invitation, actually returned as a Teacher to the very place where he had previously arrived as a poor Weaver, in search of work. He truly says: "The story of my life in Luthermuir would require a little book for itself. This I know, my efforts were graciously owned and greatly blessed by God to the people, and to me that was enough. At first I was inclined to return, but reflection led me to believe that God meant my coming, that all would be for the best. We prayed for this, and God heard us."

He had a large school, labouring hard among the young as

a teacher; helping the old in various ways—visiting, as well as lecturing, when his time and strength would permit. A valedictory address was presented to him on his leaving. From this address we give the following paragraph:—

"We need not particularize the varied offices you have so energetically fulfilled since you came here. All who have witnessed the zealous manner in which you have performed your arduous and philanthropic duties know that your great efforts have been worthy of your generous heart—the manifest good which has been effected has been graciously blessed by our heavenly Father, and now stirs a deep sense of gratitude and lasting affection in us towards you."

Thus far, one of his objects in leaving Sir George Ramsay's school was gained—that of becoming still more useful as a Christian worker, as well as a public Teacher; but he failed in the other object—becoming richer in a monetary point. In that sense he left Luthermuir poorer than he went to it. This, he in a manner admits. And, besides, he lost the benefit of Sir James's splendid library, which was kindly opened for him. Also the genial society of the Rev. Robert Hogg, of Alyth, and other kindly friends; but all this was to him more than met by the conviction that God meant his return to Luthermuir to do "a little good for it," in return for the help which it had, through some of its generous hearts, given him in times past. He believes in what he has since called "providential promptings:" He says, "For all that happened contrary to the Spirit and will of God, I feel sure he brought me back to Dundee by way of Luthermuir."

AT DUNDEE AGAIN.

In 1855, about four years after their marriage, we find the couple back to their native town. After all expenses had been paid, they had 20s. with which to meet coming claims and begin life anew. At first there was no opening for a school, and there was no time for waiting. Something had to be done, and that at once. His knowledge of medicine led him to consider the advice of some of his friends—to enter the drug trade. In making some inquiries in order to learn of a vacancy for an assistant, he was promised some bottles and medicines on credit, if a shop could be had, and this was found at the West-end, in the Perth-road, not far from the scene of former struggles in his boyhood.

He says: " The construction of the premises was such that we were able to make it our dwelling-house as well as a shop, and a large shop it was—rather too large for what we had to put in it ; but it so happened that the person who preceded me in the shop had left the counter, the shelving and gas-fittings, all ready for use. This was fortunate, as no money was required in that direction. And we were favoured with another hint which we adopted—to include books and stationery in 'the business,' receiving some things in that line 'on sale or return.'

" When we entered the shop we were reduced to 2s 6d ; and by the time we arranged our small stock and opened the door, we had one halfpenny, which we put into the till 'for luck,' as we said, smiling to each other, while the tears—indescribable emotion—dropped fast, as in prayer we said, 'God help us.' We were one, and He was with us."

They persevered, and though the reward was not great, they were thankful. The mixed business of selling boluses and books, writing paper and newspapers ultimately prospered "pretty well." And this partial success did not come a day too soon, for the domestic responsibilities soon increased—a second child arrived —" a sweet Aggie," but as tocherless as she was beautiful. As soon as the mother was again able for the two-fold task of seeing to her domestic duties and attending to matters more public behind the counter, new and special efforts had to be made. Finding that life in the country had again greatly improved his health, and thinking it possible to do in Dundee what, years before, he had done in Kerriemuir, he opened a school at the West Port—seeing to the business of the shop in the morning, *before*, and in the evening, *after*, school hours—Mrs Hillocks doing her best in the interval to supply his place.

A REMARKABLE INCIDENT.

In one sense this record of some of the leading incidents of his life, from the cradle till his entry into London, may well be called "the preparation;" but it must not be understood that his Christian efforts only date from that time. His labours of love may be said to begin when he entered public life as a teacher. And here—while, as usual, doing two men's work, he could not resist the natural impulse of his heart, to help in every good work around him, as he had opportunity, not only lecturing occasionally, but also frequently giving mission addresses in various parts of the town; and one of the meeting places to which he had been invited was in Taylor's Lane—that mission effort in connection with Free St Peter's Church, which has now developed into what is known as the M'Chyene Memorial Church, Perth Road.

He tells us: "While in the act of addressing this Taylor's Lane Mission meeting, it crossed my mind that I was standing on the very spot where, years before, I had driven the wheel. The sensation I felt was such that I paused in my discourse and related the circumstance. This brought for me a hearty round of applause. The audience evidently looked upon the incident as a triumph; and I confess I felt something of the same feeling. At all events I was filled with gratitude to God, and my hope was greatly enlivened, while my desire for higher attainment increased, that I might thereby become more useful.

WINNING A PRIZE.

It was in this Perth Road druggist shop that the prize autobiography was written. He says: "In May, 1856, a friend informed me that in February of that year prizes had been offered for the best Lives of Working Men, written by themselves, and that Professor Nichol was one of the adjudicators. He also advised me to try, even though there were only a few days in which to write. Having learned from head-quarters that I would be accepted as an eligible competitor, I tried, and in about ten sittings, after the labours of the day were over, I came to a close, bringing the life up to that time. The title of the MS. was 'The Weaver's Son,' and the motto given, instead of the name, was 'Upward and Onward.' No doubt the writers became anxious during 'the unavoidable delay caused by the examination of so much MS,' for there were nearly eighty competitors. At least I was not a little uneasy, for having consented to fight I wished to win. But I began to think that my chances were few, when I read the following sentences in the *Commonwealth* newspaper:—'We have looked carefully into the MSS. (the autobiographies), and are in a position to convey to the public the general impression we have formed of their contents. We doubt if there was ever before collected, in any shape, so large, so fresh, so varied, and so instructive a mass of information touching the condition of the working classes. They reflect, with accuracy and completeness, every circumstance of the lives of their authors and their class. The natural features are broadly, distinctly and fairly given. It has been said that romance is around us if we could see it; that comedy still laughs at births and bridals, however dull it may be on the stage; and that tragedy, whether with sceptred pall or no, has still death-beds worthy of a Shakspeare's pen. This fact has been strongly brought out in the writings before us. The gloss of the novel is rubbed off, but it is well supplied by the sterner lines of facts.'

"At last, however, my doubts were set at rest, and my joy increased, when by a kind letter I learned that my hastily-written sketch had taken a first prize."

"ON A NEWSPAPER."

But it was not long after this triumph that he was led to take one of those unfortunate steps which in the end led to all but utter disaster. Over-work, constant toils, and poor rewards brought upon him another severe illness, and this compelled him to give up teaching. After he recovered he confined himself to the shop; but though the business improved, because of his attention, the profits were not such as to enable him to make both ends meet. This pressed so heavily upon him that he felt he was unable to wait till the drugs and books might become a paying concern, and hence he the more readily accepted an engagement on a Dundee newspaper. But he was not long in office before he had reason to fear he had made a mistake—that he was far from being congenially yoked. As we have elsewhere said, his own writings were, as they still are, distinguished by a pure and high tone of morality, his political opinions being that of an independent Liberal. So far as this was concerned, things went well for a time. The arduous and trying labours did not in any way lessen his enthusiasm. But such were the causes for his repeated remonstrances that he frequently threatened to leave, unless these causes were removed—causes which gave the newspaper the scurrilous character which, in spite of his remonstrance, it ultimately attained. Finding it was useless long to press against the stream, he resigned his responsibilities, but without receiving the promised pay for the long and late hours he spent in connection with the newspaper and other duties which fell to his lot.

CHAPTER XII.

IN EDINBURGH ONCE MORE.

WHY HE LEFT DUNDEE.

"THE horse may starve while the grass is growing," was a sentence, the truth of which worked its way deeper and deeper in the heart of our hero, until he thought of giving up the Perth Road business as soon as that could be done with honour. This took place earlier than he had anticipated, because of continued depression and undue pressure. He felt convinced that the business would, in time, repay him for the money, anxiety, and care bestowed upon it, if only he could stand out "a little longer;" and hence he tried several means of help—he and his true-hearted partner labouring from early morning till late at night. But at last "the necessity of making some special effort elsewhere" became more and more evident, and yet he was reluctant to leave home, Mrs Hillocks having three children claiming her care—for he had two Maggies by this time, "Maggie the mother, and Maggie the daughter." But all things seemed to point that way, so he yielded.

For long he had been much sought for as a speaker at various meetings, children's meetings, such as Bands of Hope, and for adults at festival and other occasions. These he attended to most readily, and without any fee or reward, save the pleasure of doing good; but of late he had taken to the study of lectures more literary and historic in their nature, and better suited to literary societies—such as his "Lectures on Mrs Hemans, as a daughter, as a mother, as a poet." Also, "Sir William Wallace: lessons from his life and times." The delivery of these and other lectures, being favourably noticed by the Press, led to an invitation to give his lecture on Wallace at Leith. For this he was paid by the committee. Being favourably received by a large and respectable audience, and having promised to give another lecture on "Burns, as a Poet and a Teacher, considered in relation to the errors of his time and those of our day," he thought he might do well by attempting to push his way in Edinburgh. And the conviction that years of effort in Dundee would be almost lost was considerably modified by the hope of rising as a lecturer on moral, social, and literary subjects, and the possibility of not only obtaining an engagement on the Press, but also of getting to the college.

TOO LITTLE TO BE A POLICEMAN.

But it was not so, for some time at least. He says: "I had a few lecturing engagements, but the fact that I expected some remuneration limited their number considerably. I had something to do by way of reporting, but that was only when some one of the regular staff was ill. What I wanted was something steady to do, bringing weekly wages or a monthly salary. I sought after this as well as longed for it. For this purpose I became a reader of the *North British Advertiser*, which was to the Edinburgh people in want of work what the *Times* is to such in London. The *Advertiser* was then so placed in the window of the publishing office, George IV. Bridge, that it could be read by those who desired to avail themselves of the opportunity. There I took my turn with many others, getting as near as possible to the 'wanted' column, pencil in hand, ready to take the address where anything at all likely might be found. It was genial work that I desired, but I was willing to accept of anything honourable, however hard—even a light porter's place, though that sometimes meant the carrying of heavy burdens—for the 'situation' named in the paper was not always what the words seemed to convey. I shall only give one instance.

"I forget now what were the exact words of the 'advertisement' to which I now refer, but they were such as led me to suppose that I might be able to perform the duties required. I called, and at last saw the person named; but he at first, and somewhat abruptly, put me out of sorts by declaring there were so many applicants that he had not time to listen to the half of them. But the thought of home and home wants urged me to call again. Still thinking that the office implied the necessity of having one who was trustworthy, I gave him references as to character and all he could wish, and then added, 'surely I can perform the duties.'

"'You cannot answer *my* purpose,' he added, most emphatically, and made for off.

"'There is some mistake,' I replied, following the gentleman, determined to know what it was. I can write a fair hand; there is my notebook. I know something of business habits, and have an unstained character as to honesty and energy. What more is needed?'

"'I know all that, but you are not the *person* for me,' he added, and left.

"I became as one trying to stare through a mystery. Following him closely, I said, 'Excuse me, Sir, but tell me *why?*'

"'I'd rather not,' was the reply.

"'Perhaps you will,' I added.

"'*Well*, if you *will* have it.' But he paused, and then said, '*You—are—too—little.*'

"This shut me up. I knew, whatever I might do under

pressing want, it was impossible to add one cubit to my stature. 'Too little to write, too little to do business, too little to be honest; never, the man is crazy,' said I to myself, and then put such questions to him as led him reluctantly to solve the mystery.

"What he wanted was a man mighty in stature, to wear a long overcoat mounted with clear buttons; able, also, to wield a great cudgel; a man to stand at the bazaar door to frighten the mischievous boys. Really, after all, the gentleman was right. I was not the person for him, being too little to be a policeman."

ANOTHER "BLINK BEFORE A DRINK."

There is something laughable in this—laughable to all but those most concerned—and yet there is much that is of serious import to all who can respect struggling worth. Surely it is sad to think of such a man put to such shifts in the capital of his native country, anxious to get *any* work, especially that work for which even then he was known somewhat to be specially useful.

But at last the sunshine came—though only as "the *blink* before the drink"—and our friends were glad to be relieved, if only for a short time, from the downward pressure. In the invitation to deliver the promised lecture on "Burns as a Poet and a Teacher," his friends in Leith gave him a helping hand, not so much in what he received for the lecture, but because of the friendly notices which appeared in the *Witness* and other newspapers. The time, too, was in his favour, being shortly before the Burns' Centenary. This led him to be sought after and to be engaged by the Press on the occasion of that stirring festival, first to write descriptions of the preparations making for it, and then to report and condense the speeches made at it.

He says: "This was a windfall, and we yet rejoice in the Burns' Centenary. By it we were enabled to make another effort in the shop way—in a small way, of course, but expecting it to grow larger by degrees. This was to help to 'bring in a penny,' as my dear partner put it, for she was ever anxious to help in the onward course. It gave us a new start in life, and gave us a house instead of lodgings in which to live. The business was in the drug way as before, yet other things were added, which other things sold better than the medicine; but the locality had something to do with that."

His services were also secured in connection with "The Scottish Time-Table," then owned and published by Mr Mathers, then a prosperous newsagent. "This," Mr Hillocks remarks, "was a dry concern, dryer than the woman found the reading of the dictionary to be, she having lost the thread of the story. But it led to other things, such as the writing of the brief sketches of the leading places named in the time-table. I also assisted in the preparation of that 'Guide to Edinburgh' which Mr Mathers published.

"But that which cheered us most was the manifestation of the kindness of Messrs Johnstone & Hunter, the publishers, in connection with their truly popular and really useful monthly, *The Christian Treasury*. The work was congenial, and the firm was honourable.

"And my arrangements were such that I was enabled, when at home, to go on with my studies during a portion of the day. And even to this I consented to lecture occasionally in the evening—once more for love—for, being thus somewhat prosperous, I could not resist the opportunity of doing good in this way. My latest efforts here were the preparation and delivery of four popular lectures for the poor, on 'Home—its ties and duties.'"

OVERPOWERED AND OVERTHROWN.

As in former cases, so in this, they attended to the injunction, "Make hay while the sun shines;" but as before, too, in their anxiety to press "onward and upward," they pushed too hard—harder than they could long withstand. "Better work out than rust out" is a saying containing wholesome truth, but our friend generally carried this principle too far, even after he had several warnings. This was one of his weak points, from which he suffered often, but never more severely than at this time. He was very ill on the night on which he delivered the last of the valuable course of lectures just named. Next morning symptoms of typhus fever were more evidently telling on his exhausted frame. Another day and he had to yield, a few more and he knew not where he was nor what he was doing. Referring to this overthrow, he says:—

"My heart and pen would alike fail me were I to attempt to describe the poverty and hardships, the suffering and sorrow that followed. Somehow or other, in this respect, with us 'It never rains but it pours.' We were overpowered and overwhelmed.

"In Maggie, God had given me a skilful and careful nurse, as well as a most devoted wife—strong in that faith which soothes in sorrow and fortifies for the battle of life. But her affection and what strength she had left were never more severely tested than on this occasion. Severe and dangerous as the fever was, she entertained the hope that I would 'come through,' as she said, again and again, even when good Doctor Menzies had serious doubts. Long did she wait and watch, night and day—for there were none to help her—and it was only after the doctor's fine countenance brightened one day, as he said, 'There is a change for the better,' that she became conscious of the sad effects of her anxiety and fatigue. But after that she broke so completely down that she could scarcely walk from my bed to the door without leaning on the table or the chairs near by.

"Of course the shop was shut; none would have come even had it been possible to wait on the customers. And my other sources of income had dried up. Our little savings all gone; both now helpless; and our dear children—but I must pause. It is too hard even to think of what they must have suffered.

"Before this, calamity after calamity had come from various causes over which we had no control. As I have before said, we had known what it was to be suddenly driven from comparative comfort to positive adversity, producing pain of body and anguish of mind which cannot be described. But the past was nothing to this; yet the climax had not come. In our case 'it never rained but it poured;' so we thought, especially in relation to distress. Knowing it was useless to open the shop—even had any of us been able to attend to it—we had to remove rather than run farther in debt. As soon as we were able to creep along the streets, we went to our new abode—a wretched Potter Row garret—for we were glad to get shelter under any roof. Here we found the walls to be a mass of corruption. But there was ventilation certainly. We have seen the hailstones dancing on the rotten floor; and at night the candle would not burn because of the wind sweeping from hole to hole."

This was a "convalescent" home in philanthropic Edinburgh, and that of two who had striven hard and long to make other homes comfortable and happy. The home of our friend who at large meetings had been often rewarded by *hearty* votes of thanks, but who, at this time, would have given back all the thanks of the world if they could have purchased a crust for his loved ones.

CHAPTER XIII.

AT WORK IN THE GARRET.

FOUND IN THIS HOVEL.

IN this hovel they passed the first day of 1860. It might have seemed to be cold if not cruel irony had any one said, "A happy New-Year;" but certainly none were more in want of the kindly greeting.

That morning they had only three farthings in the world. But as a set-off against this, he says: "There was not much desire for food, we were so sore and so weak. Our trouble was more about our children than ourselves, and yet they were a blessing to us. When we looked into their sweet faces, the smiles of joy shone through the tears of gratitude. Had it not been for their sakes, we think we would have given way, the pressure was so crushing. But the next morning brought us a post-office order for one pound. Then we did not know the good lady who sent it, so we took it as a token from God that He was once more to smile upon us. We took heart again.

"'Good God! Is such a man brought to this?' said Thomas Knox, on entering our home."

This must have been a memorable scene—the abashed wife and timid children; and then the contrast between the physical condition and social position of the two men meeting one another for the first time since they parted on the platform at a meeting at which both had been cheered for their utterances. One a tall, healthy, energetic, and prosperous merchant; the other a thin, pale, trembling invalid. But though there was a marked difference in appearance, their hearts and objects were one, at least as far as the nobler features of humanity can be seen. Both desired, and had laboured, to better mankind; and even in this wretched abode the suffering invalid spent not a little of his time in the study of his favourite theme—"How to raise the poor to God and usefulness."

A HINT TO TRACT DISTRIBUTORS.

"Up to this time," he says, "this was our first visitor; but others followed, some of quite another stamp. Tract Distributors found their way up our rickety stairs, to give us a 'good advice.' Ladies as well as gentlemen came ' to enlighten' us; but the theme was much more frequently 'The wrath of God' than 'The way to Heaven.' One day one of these well-disposed ladies called. She faced the smoke and bravely entered *without being asked*, and without saying why she came. Our abode was as clean as possible; yet there was something that must have been very dismal to those who had just left a spacious drawing-room. From her conversation it was evident she put us down as 'one of the rest,' as she afterwards said—as the victims of drink and the friends of infidelity—guilty because we were poor. 'This wretched house,' she added, by way of a climax to a rather long address, ' this wretched house shows you are living under the wrath of God.'

"We listened in silence, not an easy task, but we mustered as much charity as to pity her. Having thanked her for the tract, she left, expressing a hope that we would read it. This we did, but before doing so we prayed for the 'poor' lady, that she might yet become wiser and more charitable, abler for the duties she had undertaken—those of a 'Christian Visitor.'

"The tract purported to be a sermon by the Rev. C. H. Spurgeon, who was then rising to what he has now attained. Not many hours after a gentleman called. He evidently knew of the lady's visit and the tract she left, but he was as ignorant of who we were. Having introduced the subject of the sermon, he felt it his duty, without provocation, to defend the preacher; but in such a way that I began to pity Spurgeon, convinced that he had reason to cry, 'Defend me from my friends!' It soon appeared that this visitor was a piece of pompous vanity, without a spark of Christian love, and without even the A B C of Christian knowledge. At first I was tempted to meet the fool according to his folly; but better thoughts came, and I dealt kindly with him, giving him the best advice I could—to sit at the feet of Jesus, and there learn the lessons of Faith, Hope and Charity, and when visiting the poor, to think how the sympathising Jesus would have acted, what He would have said and done.

"The visitor felt his position, but excused himself by saying, 'This is a fearful neighbourhood'—a fact which I deeply regretted."

WHY AND HOW "LIFE STORY" APPEARED.

But he tells us that they were not the only visitors, and that some were really worthy of the good work they represented. One had seen his "Thoughts in Rhyme," a book which had been in the press during the illness referred to in the last chapter, but which appeared soon after he was sufficiently recovered to revise the last sheets. "This book," he says, "was the means of helping me a little. The most of those friends who had previously ordered copies were 'as good as their word.' The critical notices, too, were such as to encourage me, if not to lead me to suppose that I was to become a poet, which, as yet, has not taken place. However, the book and the reviews of it brought my name above-board once more. But that which did far more for me in this way was the publication of my prize autobiography, now known as 'Life Story.'"

As this narrative is so closely connected with what follows, it may be interesting to the reader to know how it appeared. This we give in his own words:—

"Though the donor of the prizes, at the time they were won, gave me full liberty to do what I thought proper with my MS., yet, up to the time when we were suffering in the ruins, I had not thought of trying to derive any benefit from its publication. And perhaps I would not have done so at this time, had not the lady who had read 'Thoughts in Rhyme' suggested that I should offer it to some periodical. She said she was going to London soon, and would take my MS. to Charles Dickens, if I would bring the life up to that date.

"Thus encouraged, I made the attempt, but soon found that the work of revising and extending was difficult because I was yet very weak, and had no desk, not even a table on which to write—having had to sell all the furniture we could spare, more than we could well spare, for food. But my purpose was served by the help of a pair of old bellows placed on my knee, while I sat upon the gathered-up shake-down on which at night we rested our weary frames.

"When the lady returned from London we were disappointed, but all was not lost. Charles Dickens did not think the work suitable for his magazine, but he was pleased in his note to say a few words of commendation."

This encouragement induced him to send the note and MS. to us, asking what should be done. We believed with Dickens that the work, if published, would take well and become useful. "With this twofold assurance," he says, "I applied to the most likely booksellers for orders; and having secured as many as would cover the expenses, the autobiography was printed forthwith.

"After supplying 'the trade' and some private subscribers, I posted a few copies (1) to those who had previously shown a willingness to help me in my struggles to be useful; (2) to those for whom I entertained a high respect, especially such as had manifested an interest in behalf of the working classes; and (3) to those whom I regarded as likely to be able to help me to obtain congenial employment. And having yet one copy left of the number thus laid aside, I asked my private and faithful Counsellor to whom she thought I might send it. 'To the Queen,' was the reply. I smiled, and told her that Professor Aytoun had a day or two before offered the same suggestion, assuring me that Her Majesty would read it. This was enough. We thought there was something in it. The copy was soon wrapped in paper, and addressed 'To Her Majesty the Queen, Windsor Castle.' I also sent some copies to the Press, and anxiously, almost impatiently, did I look for the notices. I was not able to withstand a 'cutting up,' but fortunately for my weakness, I was not put to the test. The criticism was the reverse of adverse. The approval was all but unanimous. In this rare harmony there was only one jarring note, and that was after I could afford to listen to it."

"PURGING" SHAKSPEARE.

"How often," he says, "and how wonderful, too, that one thing brings about another," and then he gives an instance.

"'Is this the place where a lady called some time ago?' asked a young lady who had just left her carriage in the street to find her way to us.

"'This is the tract a lady left here lately,' I replied, offering her the sermon; but she said she had only called to have a short conversation.

"'You are the author of "Thoughts in Rhyme?"' she added, inquiringly.

"I nodded assent, and thought What more is coming?

"'You love poetry?' she said, and again I nodded assent, asking if she had seen the lines entitled 'The Happy Bard?'

"She continued, 'You prefer work to money, I understand, and have therefore brought a little work for you, and here is ten shillings to begin with,' said the lady, handing to me a large quantity of MS. copy written in a beautiful round hand.

"This good lady loved to live among the poets; and, as I understood, wished to do good by employing poor authors of poetical turn to revise and enlarge her notes on what she considered the best of the works she had read. Shakspeare was one of her favourites. She admired Macbeth and Hamlet, but thought they would be all the better if purged. And this was the work she brought for me.

"Glad as I was to get work, if only I could do it well, I did not do more than promise to read her MS. carefully. We parted to meet that day week. Only think of one with burning, aching brow and trembling hand—and eyes almost burned out by suffocating smoke—engage on the herculean task of 'purging' Shakspeare. We met on several occasions, but, at the end of three weeks—indeed before that time—I felt I was unequal to the duty, I had, by consent, imposed upon myself, to try to excise 'the objectionable features' without disjointing the sentences, weakening the force, and in some cases rendering the passage unintelligible. Indeed, I looked upon my efforts as being worthless, for any likely good, as the play of Hamlet would be with the part of Hamlet omitted. At last I told her that I could not see my way to delete what she suggested without taking away much of the strength, or lessening the beauty, or marring the sense of the whole piece, making it not only bald but incomprehensible.

"I admitted the truth of much that she lamented; but I tried also to convince her that Shakspeare, take him all and all, was comparatively pure, comparing his plays with many presented in connection with what was called 'the Dramatic Art.' I strove to point out that his diction was as simple as his thoughts were lofty; to show her that such was generally the case whether we read his descriptions of every grade of life, from the cradle to the grave, we see in him a never-failing artist, who had been taught by the Word and the Works of God as well as by the ways of men and women of all times. Having also called her attention to the fact that the Great Poet was by far the grandest and the most powerful when he had Bible pictures before his mind—and when his mind was filled with Bible sentiments—I at last ventured to point out to her several ways in which she might be more useful. One was to write on the point contained in the last sentence, giving the passages from both books. Another was to give an improved edition of the 'Beauties of Shakspeare,' expanding on the moral inculcated.

"At our last interview she thanked me for being so candid and attentive, and then gave me another ten shillings for my labour. The money was acceptable, and the effort had in it its own reward."

CHAPTER XIV.

THE LAST OF HIS SCOTTISH STRUGGLES.

IN THE PROFESSOR'S CHAIR.

HE adds, what must be very pleasant to hear, "The study of Shakspeare under no end of difficulties was the means of helping us out of the hovel, and I need not say we were glad. As yet, our furniture was very scanty, and our table did not groan under its load, but we were thankful. I well remember the thoughts that passed through my mind when sitting at the first meal in our new home. Even Jeanie, the baby—only a few weeks old—seemed to enjoy the relief with us; her lovely face looked all the lovelier. Six human beings, each having a destiny; I was overcome as I thought; then all, save baby, wept, but more in joy than sorrow.

"Our removal was not an hour too early. We soon found, though we had left the Potter Row ruins, its sad effects on our frames had not left us. But this was more manifest in George, our dear boy and only son. 'The poor lad, he has had a hundred chances to one against his young life,' said the doctor, after he saw that the turn for the better had come.

"God is ever working, making all things work together for good to those that love Him; but we do not always see that working while it is going on. During this new trial we were not a little cast down, but God was supporting and blessing all the time. Old friendships were being renewed and new ones were being formed. Our minister, the Rev. Dr Reid, of the

Lothian Road United Presbyterian Church, was as kind as ever, as also the late Professor Miller; while Professors Aytoun and Blackie manifested a desire to help me for the ministry. The warm-hearted Greek scholar generously presented me with an honorary order giving me all the advantages of his Greek classes at the University. This he did as a mark of his respect 'for persevering endeavours to rise to usefulness.'

"This was a kind offer, well meant, and gladly did I avail myself of the privilege as often and as long as my circumstances would permit. 'Another step,' said I to myself, 'the better to prepare me for the object of my life.' It was so. But the good man also did us the honour to call at our humble home —'to see Auntie Maggie and the *bairnies;*' and such was his kindly Christian way of consoling and encouraging us that it soon became evident that he knew human nature as well as Greek. He was as cordial and hearty as if we had been his equal in station and learning. He, on leaving, invited me to his residence to have 'an extended conversation.' Pleasant and profitable were the hours I spent with him and his kind lady. One day he asked me to meet him in an apartment adjoining his class room. We arrived at the College together, he leading me to the apartment named. He then left me alone, but it was not long before he returned in gown and cap, ready for work. 'Come this way,' was the next injunction. I obeyed, and in a few seconds we were on the rostrum facing the great mass of students. Addressing me he said, 'You must either deliver the lecture or occupy the chair.' This was followed by one of those shouts of applause which only students can give. And those who know the Professor are aware how enjoyably he could do such. I felt bewildered, and my face was not pale then; but he soon explained all by introducing me as the author of 'a piece of real life,' called 'Life Story,' following this remark up by an earnest and eloquent panegyric amplifying the ideas expressed in a letter to me in relation to that little book.

Though I felt very queer in my rather elevated position, I had this consolation—I could say what many of our A.M.'s, LL.D.'s, D.D.'s, and other College dons could not say—I had been unexpectedly and unanimously called to fill the professorial chair of one of the proudest and best universities of the world. But there was little time to spare for such thoughts, for my mind, like that of others, was soon trying to follow the Professor in his grand and eloquent lecture. For the time all else was forgotten."

BECOMES A MISSION TEACHER.

This was very kind on the part of Professor Blackie, and the benefit of attending his classes has not been lost; but our friend also became a *bona fide* professor in a college where he has ever been at home, where he taught and learned. At the request of a few ladies interested in the poor, he also became what was called a " Mission Teacher," as well as the student.

As usual, and before he was fully restored, he must have double work. It has been said his error was in having too many irons in the fire, and we have thought so, too; but generally they were necessary, because of the circumstances, as in this instance. Food for the mind, culture and information, are useful, but the body must also be seen to, and domestic claims must be met; hence it was that he at this time readily undertook this work, even when yet very weak, the effects of the fever.

"To this peculiar work," he says, "I devoted as much time and strength as I could give before and after—and sometimes between—the university classes. The pupils of whom I took charge were not assembled in the ordinary schoolrooms; but in any of the most suitable apartments available in any of the lowest places of the city, and among the most wretched of its people—sometimes in a back kitchen, and sometimes in a rickety attic. The scholars were understood to be little children, but it was soon found that children of a larger growth came to listen. Half an hour was the time appointed for one class and one room, and that only once a day. And this enabled me to go over a large number in the course of a week.

"In one sense my task was unpleasant, the people were so poor, and I had neither food nor clothing, gold nor silver, to give them; but I could add, 'such as I have, give I thee'—sympathy and effort. But though the condition of the places was as sad as the poverty of the people, I loved the work for the sake of the poor, and because I felt sure God's blessing attended my labours. And besides, I was taught much that has not been forgotten. This work, coming so soon after my own sad experience, and while I was yet suffering not a little, perhaps, made me feel more deeply for those I visited; hence I could not take it easy, as kind friends would sometimes suggest. I did my best for the spiritual welfare of the adults, as well as the children, not forgetting the physical and intellectual condition in which I found them."

"TOO LITTLE" ONCE MORE.

"Truly, if my family could have been supported by what I had for this work, I could have given my life to it; but that was impossible, the income thereby only being a very few shillings weekly."

In these words we see the bent of his mind—that he was not merely willing but very anxious to avail himself of every likely opportunity to labour for the happiness of his fellow-creatures. But they also tell us the reason why he wished to improve the comfort of his home while striving to be useful. Two offers of other work had come—the Editorship of a Scottish newspaper and a Reportership on a London newspaper—and fain would he have tried, especially in the latter case, to benefit his position; but his friend, Dr Menzies, assured him he was yet too weak to venture from home and engage in such work. But about that time a kind-hearted friend—the Secretary to the Soldier's Friend Society—informed him that such services as he could render were wanted by that Society in the Castle of Edinburgh. "The very thing," he said to himself; and, acting on advice, he lost no time in forwarding an application for the vacant situation to the London Board. Among the testimonials which he enclosed was one from his minister, in which he stated that Mr Hillocks possessed the talent of exhibiting Divine Truth in a form fitted to interest, "and was otherwise peculiarly qualified to commend the Gospel;" that he was "a man of great energy and industry, ever anxious to discharge his duties faithfully." He also added that he "admired the resignation" which the applicant had "manifested under severe and accumulated afflictions."

The decision of the London Board was all that could be desired, and hopes were raised; but the Chaplain had yet to be satisfied. "This," he says, "was the stumbling-block, the Chaplain would not be satisfied. A friend asked him why he did not accept of my services in the Scripture Readership, and the reply was, 'He is too little to speak to my tall men!' But certainly this was not the only reason. When I had the *honour* of a conversation with this man in *high* authority (he was not much taller than I was), he said, 'You are a Dissenter, I understand, and the question is, Are you a Dissenter *on principle?*' He emphasised the two last words. 'I am,' was the reply, and we parted. I asked myself the question—'When shall the time come that those who have the will shall not have the power thus to manifest the worst form of Sectarianism?'"

WORDS OF CHEER.

But this disappointment was somewhat modified by the kindness of others and the words of cheer which came in letters sent to him from all parts of the United Kingdom. He says: "I can scarcely refrain from naming a few who wrote to me after reading 'Life Story.' The letters from the Duke of Argyle, the Right Hon. Lord Kinnaird, the late Sir George Ramsey, Sir John Ogilvey, George Kinloch, Robert Chambers, Duncan M'Laren, M.P., Thomas Cooper, were kindly and encouraging, well calculated to keep hope alive. 'Go on in the strength of God'—'I commend you and yours to God'—'Excelsior is your motto, stick to it'—'God will make way for you and provide for your good wife and dear children.' Such were a few of the cheerful words sent to us. Often have I read the letters, and as often have I thanked God and the writers. But the letter which, at that time, increased and strengthened our hopes of being soon relieved from that rather severe pinching which accompanies a small income, was from the pen of Lord Brougham. He promised to do what he could to further my desires—to get congenial work—when he saw Mr Hastings, then the Secretary of the Social Science Association. But this was not the way God was opening up for me.

Some time after this, and while preparations were making for the second edition, a very kind letter came from the Right Hon. W. E. Gladstone, showing that he had read the little book with the greatest care. The value of his generous and thoughtful 'expression of sympathy' and of 'admiration' was greatly enhanced by the questions he asked in relation to some of the incidents merely alluded to in the book. This gave me an opportunity of giving a full explanation, with which the great Statesman was 'perfectly satisfied.'"

CHAPTER XV.

A TRIBUTE—DEPARTED FRIENDS.

ALL this was encouraging, and he was grateful. This gratitude he is not slow to express, as may be gathered from some of his brief sketches of those whose friendship he enjoyed—sketches of the living as well as the dead; but we shall select four of those who have gone to their rest above. But while we confine ourselves to these, as showing his sincere attachment, as well as his hearty appreciation of talent and goodness in others, it is well, also, to bear in mind that there are other friends still here below whose character and ability he admires and appreciates; such, for instance, as our esteemed friend, William Logan, of Glasgow, the editor of that most valuable work, "Words of comfort to parents bereaved of little children," and to whom Mr Hillocks appropriately dedicated his "Welfare of Children." Of Mr Logan it may well be said, as the Vicar of Wakefield said of Newberry, the bookseller, "he is a friend of all mankind," particularly of struggling worth and genius. His paternal conduct to poor David Gray, the Poet of the Luggie, is itself enough to perpetualize his name. Having heard of Mr Hillocks as a speaker and writer on social subjects, viewed from the Christian standpoint, Mr Logan sent him a copy of his "Moral Statistics of Glasgow." This was the commencement of their friendship.

THOMAS LAMB.

In connection with the subject already referred to in Chapter IX., he thus speaks of Mr Lamb as one who had a considerable interest in him as in others of the same literary circles:

"Like many others, I owe much to the Dundee Literary Societies. They were to me valuable schools, in which I learned much that has been very useful to me in every walk of life wherein I have trodden—awakening that love of literature which has since grown with my years—preventing me from ever being alone if a book is in the way and I be able to think. But I would be very ungrateful if I could leave this subject without saying that not a little of our lasting pleasure and fruitful benefits are due to the thoughtful generosity of our fatherly friend, the late Thomas Lamb. Little did the good man think what a boon he was conferring on society, far beyond Dundee, when he was making it one of the chief objects of his life to encourage and guide the more intelligent young men in mutual advancement. The many travellers who have occasion to put up in Dundee—especially that large and useful class known as the 'gentlemen of the road'—have reason to rejoice in the grand consummation of that noble enterprize—that useful monument of unaided industry and steady perseverance in Reform-street —known as Lamb's Temperance Hotel—*an establishment true to its name;* but none have more reason to express their gratitude to our late worthy citizen, Thomas Lamb, than the large number who, about the time to which I now refer, were members of the literary societies which found a home in 'The Halls of Lamb.' It is *there*, in the Murray-gate Rooms, our associations centre. It was *there* where our temperance and temperate landlord became and continued to be our patron, our counsellor, our father. And he was Mr Lamb throughout—his worthy partner in life and their amiable daughter assisting him. Our pleasant re-unions, prolonged debates, or stormy meetings, found him ready for the occasion. Though in our highest keys of fun and frolic, we sometimes tested his patience rather severely, yet all was right by the next meeting; the same happy welcome and inviting comfort were ready for all—even the wildest of the madcaps—and with few exceptions, we were wild enough when we made up our minds for fun. He knew we meant no harm, and he took care that we did no harm. He ruled in love and we yielded in love—that is, when we in fun had gone too far."

ALEXANDER LAING, THE BRECHIN POET.

It was not long after this that Alexander Laing, the author of "Wayside Flowers"—in a very pleasant letter—opened the way to what became "another of the warm and valuable friendships." Mr Hillocks says: "From the moment I read that letter, I felt sure the writer was a genial, kindly poet, an intelligent, manly Christian. But it was not till I was teacher in Luthermuir that I had the pleasure of seeing him face to face.

" 'I have come seven miles to see you on this hot summer day,' said my reverend-looking friend, who had, by a hearty knock, called our attention to the schoolhouse door; ' but you do not know me. I am from Brechin, and my name is Alexander Laing. Do I see the " Young Weaver?" ' No farther introduction was needed. He was soon seated, and we spent quite an hour over our tea. It was a delightful hour. He presented to me a copy of his 'Wayside Flowers.' The inscription on the fly-leaf was written in a peculiar but readable hand.

" 'Now, my young friend, I must tell you that "gif-gaff mak's gude freen's." I have a copy of your "Passages in the Life of a Young Weaver," but I wish one from *you* with my name and your name upon it, *written by you*,' said the author of 'Archy Allan,' with one of those pawky, sweet smiles that belonged to himself and which gave point to what he said. I felt as much honoured as I was gladdened by this request. Ere this I had questioned myself as to the propriety of offering the dear, good man a copy of that little production; but I could not, till the request was thus made, venture to exchange the compliment by giving the 'Weaver' for the 'Flowers.'

"'What a gem!' said Mrs Hillocks, as the tall, thin, neatly attired form of the poet was returning home; 'so kind and kindly, so quiet and cheerful, so modest yet manly. His wife must be happy in him, he is so full of God and goodness.'

"My beloved was right. He was a gem then in preparation for the Saviour's crown, in which he is now set. But this visit was only an earnest of the treat that followed. For nights we studied 'flower' after 'flower,' now weeping and now laughing. The poetry of the fireside came home to us. It was so simple, so true, and characterised throughout by a high moral tone, as well as real poetic merit. It brought before us the time past as if yet present, when

> 'The brae o' the burnie a' blooming in flower,
> An' twa faithfu' lovers mak' ae happy hour.'

I could see for myself, and rejoice in the sight of

> 'A kind, winsome wifie, a clean, canty hame,
> A smilin' sweet babie, to lisp the dear name.'

I knew what he meant when he sung—

> 'I wadna gi'e my ain wife for ony wife I see,
> For O, my dainty ain wife, she's aye so dear to me;
> A bonnier yet I've never seen, a better canna be—
> I widna gi'e my ain wife for ony wife I see.'

And both of us could see the truth and the beauty in the lines which the artist has illustrated, and which picture has been called by the name the poet's volume bears—

> 'There's a moral, my child, in the wayside flower;
> There's an emblem of life in its short-lived hour;
> It smiles in the sunshine, and weeps in the shower,
> And the footsteps fall on the wayside flower.
> Now see, my dear child, in the wayside flower,
> The joys and the sorrows of life's passing hour.
> Yet know, my dear child, that the wayside flower
> Shall revive in its season, and bloom its brief hour;
> That again we shall blossom in beauty and power,
> Where the foot never falls on the wayside flower.'

We were charmed, and in his after letters to us we found much of the same warm-heartedness, generous emotions, deep sense of human nature, and thorough trust in God—ever fresh, fervent, and consistent."

WITH THE "CHRISTIAN PHILOSOPHER."

"It was while in Broughty Ferry that our friend first met Thomas Dick, "the Christian Philosopher." He was a frequent visitor to the shop, not for medicine, but to have "short chats" with the druggist. "Our conversations," Mr Hillocks remarks, "were encouraging as well as instructive. Knowing my aims, and seeing the difficulties in my way, he would cheer me somewhat, by giving me some details of his own life, pointing out what he called the parallel passages, especially in the early parts of our lives, and I could not help seeing eye to eye with him so far.

"For instance, he would say, 'We were both brought to life in the *Hill*town (Dundee). Born to climb, not merely the *little hills*, but the great hill of difficulty. And though poor, we are rich. Both fathers had liberal and benevolent views of the character and grace of God—a rich inheritance.'

"He also told me that when nine years of age, an incident

occurred—the appearing of the celebrated meteor, August 18, 1783—which had much to do with the special bent of his mind. From that time he lived nearer to God—'among the stars.' It was, he would remind me, when I was about the same age that I saw the light for the first time. It did not burst upon my view so clearly as did the meteor light upon his; but I, too, was astonished and arrested, not in fear, but in joy, and from then the tendency of my mind has been upward. From that year (1783) he was led to think and speak of the stars and our Maker, for his studies were religious as well as scientific—he sought to show the goodness as well as the greatness of God in the works of Creation. And I, too, had been led to think and speak of the Bright and the Morning Star rising with healing on His wings.

"Again, he thought no shame to tell me that he, too, was once a weaver, his eyes following the lines of some favourite book while his feet kept the treadles in motion, and his hand made the shuttle fly from side to side. Also becoming a teacher as I had. But here, as I told him, the parallel ended; and even at the beginning there was an important difference. *His* father was able to help him not only to books and glasses, but also to the *regular* curriculum of a student of divinity. Still I felt interested in the story of his valuable life—how he was licensed to preach in 1801, having previously contributed several essays to various publications; how he continued to teach and to write, prosecuting his astronomical researches, and at last publishing his 'Christian Philosopher.' How he removed to Broughty Ferry in 1827, and built the neat cottage on the rugged brow of a barren hill, 'with the view of holding closer communion with God and the stars.' How he sought to Christianize science by constantly diffusing his very extensive and most accurate knowledge of astronomy, not only by his prolific pen, but also availing himself of opportunities to speak wherever he was invited by any Christian denomination;

never permitting sectarianism to stand in the way of his usefulness. How he published his 'Philosophy of the Future State' in 1828. How the degree of LL.D. was conferred upon him in 1832, the diploma being sent to him from New York free of expense. How he visited London, Paris, and other important cities, where not a few distinguished privileges were accorded to him. How, about the same time, 1837, he published his 'Celestial Scenery,' and how he employed his spare moments in benevolent labours of love, quietly, but truly usefully.

"It was when thus engaged that I had the pleasure of first meeting him and sharing his valuable friendship, for which I thank God to this day."

DR GUTHRIE OF EDINBURGH.

When Mr Hillocks thought of making Edinburgh his home in the hope the better to obtain the object he had in view, we gave him an introductory note to Alexander Smith, John Gorrie, and others, and though they had not the pleasure of helping him to work as they desired, yet he rejoiced in having met them, more especially the poet, of whom he speaks in hearty praise. And the same may be said in relation to another poet, Thomas Aird. With both he was on intimate and friendly terms; but the prose poet most genial to his own aspirations was the Rev. Thomas Guthrie, of Edinburgh.

It will be remembered that in referring to the dangerous illness of his son, Mr Hillocks expressed the conviction that "God was blessing all the time," and no doubt he had in his mind the helpful kindness which afterwards sprung from one of the friendships that was formed soon after this affliction. He says: "One of the ladies who heard of the illness of our dear boy, and who called to see him, was Miss Guthrie, the Doctor's daughter, and she—together with 'Life Story'—led to my receiving a hearty invitation to one of her father's breakfast gatherings.

"Ere this I had heard of the great fame of this good man; of the Christian philanthropy which he threw into all his undertakings in the midst of the 'Sins and Sorrows' of the city wherever need had roused his sympathy. Frequently had I seen his tall form on errands of mercy where few of the rich and famous were seen—where the festering dens of vice abound, in the Canongate, the High Street, and the Grass Market. I had also listened with admiration to his thrilling eloquence when every one of the spell-bound audience were being charmed to duty as the orator spoke from the heart to the heart—his noble example giving point to his persuasive power. But it was not until I had the invaluable pleasure of his cheering presence and bracing friendship that I felt the sweet influence of his loving character; it was on the occasion of our very first interview that I felt his presence was as stimulating as it was friendly—the man to help another to work and weep for the poor and the wretched.

The breakfast party was large and lively. Some of the guests were from abroad, but all were at home. The Doctor's fund of humorous and telling anecdote was as exhaustless as his knowledge of men and manners was great—every sentence he uttered indicated a deep insight into human nature—incidentally, but clearly, revealing the cheering fact that his large heart, like his great work, was in the vineyard of humanity. That Christian humanity which prompts endeavours to ameliorate the condition of every class—the suppression of cruelty and the manifestation of gentleness—uplifting the fallen and bearing their burdens—rescuing the orphans, and the worse than orphans, the neglected Arabs, from the gutter and starvation, to new life, and comfort, and hope—enlarging and exalting the mind—and all by the use of the means which God is sure to bless to the saving and raising of man through Christ crucified.

"The subjects of conversation were various, and though the

Doctor was ready for whatever turned up, yet he was evidently more at home in his own special field of usefulness. Speaking of the necessity of exposing evil, he held that true men and women were not contaminated with the atmosphere in which they saw it to be their duty to live and work, and that contact with the victims of wrong did not harden the heart, as had been said. To prove his position, he named an incident connected with one of Thackeray's visits to Edinburgh. 'One Sabbath afternoon,' said the Doctor, 'this fearless fellow was going down the Canongate, when his attention was called to three almost naked children at a *close* end, their feet red as *collops*, yet singing " There is a happy land, far, far away." This scene,' added the Doctor, 'was too much for Thackeray. It opened the floodgates of the large heart of the great author. He wept like a child.'"

"After breakfast I was favoured with a private interview, which the Doctor kindly suggested, to learn in what way he could help me to work more remunerative. He gave me a note of introduction to Mr Troup, who had just succeeded Mr Peter Bayne in the editorship of the Edinburgh *Witness* newspaper. This caused Mr Troup to take a deeper interest in 'Life Story,' so much so that he sent his copy to a friend in London, the Rev. J. H. Wilson, already named. But this was only the first of several interesting interviews with the Doctor, and the first of many valuable letters from him. His letters were generally short, but always full of hearty sympathy, cheering encouragement, or wise counsel—ever manifesting an affectionate interest in my work, and a fatherly care in the worker. At times they took the form of notes of warning, approaching to a kindly scolding. Well he knew the likely results of what he called 'giving way to my weak point—forgetting that even the strongest frame cannot withstand continuous work almost night and day.'

"On one occasion, however, he let slip the fact that it was

easier, under such circumstances, and on such a point, to preach than it was to practise. Ill as I was, I laughed right out. He had heard that I was laid aside by labouring beyond my strength, and he summed up a very loving rebuke by the apt injunction —'Do thyself no harm.' This was all very well, but I only read a few lines more when, in relation to his own health and efforts, he said—'I have been killing myself for the last six weeks pleading the cause of a glorious mission.'

"So anxious was he that I should be careful, that he would sometimes prove the necessity of following his advice by giving the weight of his experience. On another occasion, urging me to accept a call to the ministry in the country, for a time at least, he said—'I know what such city work as yours is. I had years of it, and it is a burden both on mind and body—a strain on the nervous system greater than any can stand beyond a certain limit.'

CHAPTER XVI.

MORE STEPPING-STONES TO LONDON.

AN IMPORTANT DECISION.

BUT during these interviews with Dr Guthrie and others, he was still plodding on as the Mission Teacher and eager student. Nor was his pen idle, for it was about this time that he wrote the letters headed, "The Homes of the Poor, by one who lived in them." They appeared in one of the Edinburgh daily newspapers, and attracted considerable attention, leading those in authority to see for themselves what he had described. He also wrote an article on the same subject for *Tait's Magazine*. Yet—as was natural and proper—he was anxiously waiting an opening by which his family might become a little more comfortable. This was brought more closely home to him by a letter from London written by the Rev. J. H. Wilson, who, having read the copy of the little book Mr Troup sent him, wrote to say, "The author is not altogether unknown to me. I see he is still aspiring to the ministry, and I shall be glad to use what influence I may have to help him in that direction." This was soon followed by another letter to Mr Hillocks, conveying the same idea, but thoughtfully adding, that what influence he had was "centred with those known as the Congregationalists."

"This," says our friend, "led me to remember what had transpired years ago, and to tell Mr Wilson, in reply, how when the Dundee teacher, I had met with the Rev. Mr Just, then the Congregational minister at Newport, Fife; how he had given me a copy of the principles held by his denomination; how, later on, I had some correspondence on that matter with the Rev. Dr W. L. Alexander, Edinburgh; how the theme had been the subject of several conversations with my minister—one of the conversations being so late as only a week previous; and how he then commended the course suggested, should Providence be pleased to give the opportunity—giving an instance of a young man who by making such a change became very useful in the ministry.

"Of course my loving and lovable pastor was careful to remind me that it was necessary to see that the conscience was clear in such matters, and that such a step naturally involved a most careful and prayerful consideration of the whole case in its special and personal bearing. And I need not say that such wholesome advice was readily taken. Though past experience had proved the possibility of my being able to unite in Christian work with the earnest and liberal workers of all denominations, yet no inducement—not even the offer of situations promising increasing usefulness, far less pecuniary benefits—had drawn me from that portion of the Church of Christ to which I was so early and warmly attached. But now, thought I, the time may soon come when I shall have to say 'Yes' or 'No' in relation to the removal to another corner of the vineyard. And when I came closer to the point I could see no sacrifice of principle in making any such change —nothing at least to trouble me. So far as I could see, the leading difference was in the matter of Church government —very important in its way—but I could see much that was good in both, in 'Presbyterianism' and 'Congregationalism.'

"Having thought so, I said so in my letter to Mr Wilson, adding, I would most gladly come south should Providence enable him to give me the opportunity."

A VALUABLE LETTER.

We refer to the Queen's letter to Mr Hillocks—a letter which he regards as important in more ways than one. Then such letters were not so frequently seen as they are now; but it was not so much in the light that he had been specially favoured that he saw the value of this letter—though certainly there is something in the thought of a little book, from the pen of one then so far reduced in the social scale, being so carefully read at the palace as to cause inquiries to be made concerning the author. It is possible its closing words specially riveted the attention of Her Majesty. They are very touching: "Reader, for the present we part. Mine is the sad story of one who has not passed the prime of life, but of one who is as anxious as ever to be useful; of one who, though he has not reached the 'far up height,' is yet as willing as ever to climb the steep, however difficult." This simple statement of a thrilling fact could not but move the tender heart of one who had read what preceded it, and doubtless this had something to do in calling forth the interesting letter which Her Majesty indited and sent to the author But we prefer giving his thoughts on the matter in his own words.

"I know the Queen's letter to me had a value far beyond the pecuniary honorarium, the five pounds sent 'as a mark of appreciation.' To one situated as I was, that was a great and timely help. Only think of the happy children handling the five sovereigns while their parents were reasoning as to the best purpose to which they could be put. 'Perhaps they will help us to London,' said the mother, and the tears ran down her cheeks.

"Yes, this was something; but there was more than this—there was the peculiar wording of the letter to be considered in relation to the circumstances by which we were and had been surrounded. Whatever else may be said of poverty, it is not unjust to it to say, it rouses suspicion. And then there are the inventions of the wicked, too often adopted by the thoughtless, frequently ending in giving to 'airy nothing a local habitation and a name.' I know it is said that the blame of certain people is praise in the eyes of others. And that is true. So far as these two classes are concerned, one is pretty safe, even though poor; but there are others—the middle ones—whose opinions and words have a considerable weight, and on whose ears evil reports may so fall as to lead them to say to their neighbours, 'Who would have thought it?' And these neighbours have other friends whose ears are also open to catch whatever is going and growing, which something—however petty or groundless to begin with—is caught up and eagerly retailed with all attention to the fullest possible particulars, the baneful influence telling more and more on the slandered victim.

"This has been the case with many; perhaps with all the poor of this earth who—fearing God, fear none beside—have had the courage earnestly and fearlessly to war against the vices of the day.

"Such at least we thought. And besides, neither of us had any sympathy with those who affected to be regardless of what any one might say of them. The truth is, we would rather be in favour with man, when that is compatible with Christian principle and practice. This, whenever realised, assisted our usefulness and enhanced our happiness; but we found that poverty, as viewed by many, bears down against this natural and proper desire. In the most crushing poverty, as in comparative prosperity—amid struggles and temptation—care was taken to maintain an irreproachable character, and God had helped us through good report and in bad report; yet frequently we had been stung by the meeting of one and another whose heart had been *once* all right towards us—whose former kindness had been evident, and whose friendship we had valued —but who, because of the poisonous breath of 'viperous slander,' had suddenly become so cold as to freeze the heart. To us this was galling, and we felt it keenly, because such a state of things existed, and because we feared lest our desired usefulness had been lessened in proportion as the preventible suffering had thereby been increased. And the thoughts likely to arise in connection with such a conviction—based on sad experience—were not altogether driven from our minds when this letter came to hand. But lately restored from the bed of affliction, every penny gone, no income, and forsaken by nearly all with whom I had previously co-operated in labours of love, some having done so intentionally—first, because of the dangerous nature of the fever, and then because it left me poor and helpless. To others who were above such causes, especially the latter, we were lost because we crept out of the way. This was evident from what such did for us after they found us in the hovel. But though some of the salt of the earth, those with whom faith, hope, and charity were more than mere words, had once more favoured me with their warm sympathy; yet the chilling trail of the crushing effects of poverty was there. I could not help feeling that the pale face, the feeble step and the sorry dress had something to do with not a few who passed by on the other side, as if I had committed some crime, while God knew I was the same man in faith, hope and charity as when we met on the platform or in the committee-room —perhaps, after all, a little nearer God—at least as anxious as ever to serve Him.

"Such slights, I fear, were the result of poverty, and slander on the part of the wicked and the thoughtless—the latter adhering too rigidly to the Scotch saying, 'There must be water where the stirk is drowned.' Hence I rejoiced in this letter, and was thankful because of the 'Scotch caution' of our good Queen in making 'inquiries,' and because Her Majesty was graciously pleased to bear testimony that the inquiries made 'proved perfectly satisfactory.'

"But there is another reason why I put special value on this letter. In its way it was one of the stepping-stones to London. With me, worshipping rank and titles *as such*, goes against the grain. I admit and admire the manifestations of well-sustained rank; but history has shown that high station may become a great power for mischief, as it always does when true principle is absent. Hence it is a source of delight and comfort to all concerned when grace and glory are blended; when those in high places prove that by God's help the august and the serene may be united; when true moral greatness gives that pleasing, placid dignity which befits one in authority and fills the people with confidence—leading on and up to that general and sincere admiration which our Queen enjoys—because of her personal virtues, and because she is a true woman as well as a careful Sovereign. Hence a confiding people take notice of and delight in the smaller things of common life as well as the greater things of State; and no doubt this accounted partly for the increasing interest which the Press—from the *Court Circular* to the local journal—took in the little book. At all events, it led many to read it a second time; and one of those who did so was the Editor of the *Witness*, who was so interested in the autobiography that he sent a copy to his friend in London, and so formed another link in the events which latterly led me on from the capital of Scotland to the capital of England—a result which could not have been anticipated, but which clearly shows that a gracious Providence is pleased to bless the right use of the proper means—even the ordinary human instrumentality."

A PASSING REMARK.

"Who can tell the worth of timely help—what it may do for good, or what evil it may prevent? Many, even of the honest poor, have missed their way, and some have fallen, from the want of the necessary assistance at the proper time. And, alas! when they do fall, how few, even of the virtuous, rise again? Help may come too late, or the proffered assistance may not be suitable. Let those who have the power to help, think, and think in time."

These are thoughtful words drawn from sad experience. They bring the reader back to the time when he found he was "too little to be a policeman," and could not find work more suited to his mind and training. Certainly it would have been a ridiculous sight to see our friend arrayed in "*long* overcoat," mounted with clear buttons, doing duty as a Beadle; but it would not have been much more out of place—though, perhaps, much less congenial—than Burns serving as a Gauger. Notwithstanding the boasted advance of our day, and its affected readiness to assist aspirants in their upward way, it is to be feared that cases of hard struggling and ill-requited merit—such as that before us—are probably not much less numerous than they were in the poet's time.

Doubtless this, like much that is wrong, rises more from " the want of thought than the want of heart." Some seem to imagine that patronage in every form is an evil—restraining power and deadening genius. From this we beg leave to differ. It certainly goes in the teeth of the practice of many communities. In Germany and in France, far more than in Britain, genius and worth have become the pass-port to wealth and honour. Nor do we believe this has tended to degrade the possessors—it has certainly given them more leisure, and led to more elaborate and useful undertakings. For instance, what a contrast between Burns dying in neglect, and ere he had reached the prime of life, in his poor Dumfries hovel, and Goethe—in nature inferior in some points to his—living long, loaded with honours, and allowed to complete his culture and his splendid poems. Was Milton, whose excellence was of the very highest order, a whit the worse for being promoted by Cromwell? Do we reward with large fortunes and splendid titles our Wellingtons—men of great powers, but who seem to a large class of the community little else than magnificent homicides—and shall we haggle about paltry sums to the benefactors of the species? How many—like the late excellent Dr Dick, of Broughty Ferry—have been compelled by narrow circumstances to part for a trifle with the copyright of valuable works? We are sure all who knew the "Christian Philosopher" were glad to hear of his receiving a slice, however small, of the Queen's pension money.

In saying this, we do not mean that our friend's case had in it a marked parallel to the cases given. He was yet young in years and struggling to rise. He had advanced somewhat, but had not risen to eminence sufficient to demand attention. Yet, as one not only in "the pursuit of knowledge under difficulties," but also anxious to give himself to that sphere of life so much wanted in that proud city, and every large city, surely it was sad to see him so often disappointed and suffering so severely. And this the more so, when we know how little it required to help him to rise to increasing usefulness. The least help to ease the burden and the oppressed one rebounds.

CHAPTER XVII.

THOUGHTS ON LEAVING FOR LONDON.

THE THOUGHT OF PARTING WITH HOME AND FRIENDS.

THE invitation came, Mr Wilson having sent to say that a very suitable sphere was open if Mr Hillocks could find his way to London that week; so there was no time to spare. He says: "It nearly took my breath away. I was almost choked with mingled emotions—because of the invitation, and the difficulty of getting away. It was soon very evident that our circumstances would not permit Mrs Hillocks and our children then to accompany me to London; and the thought of leaving them behind pressed heavily on my mind.

"This may be called mere sentimentality, and I have no wish to question the statement. As has been said, 'one might have supposed that all such emotional tenderness' might have been lashed out of me ere this. Not so, however. One of the effects of the 'lashing' seemed to rouse rather than subdue such emotions; and, perhaps, never before were the strength of the family feelings more evident than now. I ever believed, with the poet, that

> 'To make a happy fireside clime
> For weans and wife,
> Is the true pathos and sublime
> Of human life.'

Along with the wish to be able to help the helpless, strengthen the weak, and raise the fallen, had grown the ever-present desire to see my home comfortable and my loved ones happy, considering these to be the most important of our Christian duties to God and man. And this is well. A man's character is not only best known at home, his general usefulness—more especially in evangelistic work—greatly depends on the nature of the domestic circle from which he goes forth to labour. This I know, whatever have been my difficulties in the world, whatever my struggle for life, whatever have been the nature of the duties I have had to attend to, whatever the responsibilities I have had to sustain, whatever the dangers I have had to encounter, in whatever spirit I have gone up to them—whether that of courage or kindness—all, under God, was greatly and happily influenced by home-help, from the heroic 'mother *at home*,' and our dear 'buds of promise' there. Ah, yes, the precious gems which God had given me enlivened and beautified our poorest abode. The love, the care, and the counsel of my 'better-half' were so blessed by God that to them I owe the strength and success which He—in His providence and by His grace—has been pleased to give me, helping me to speak and act with cheerful energy under the most trying circumstances. A gifted partner, a brave companion, a true-hearted woman, a skilful nurse, an affectionate mother, a loving wife. Truly, I had reason to thank God for 'Maggie and our pets.' And hence the reluctance to leave them even for a short time. But here, too, she was helpful in reminding me of what, for the time, I had almost forgotten. 'You know,' she said, 'God is everywhere present—in Edinburgh and in London—a very present help in every time of trouble, and nigh unto all them that call upon Him.'

"This was enough. But then came my last round as a Mission Teacher, and the parting with my scattered charge, many of whom really loved me. My salary—if the few shillings which I received weekly could be called by that name—was very small, but that was not my only remuneration. There was the pleasure which comes of the conviction that good is being done—in helping the poor to make the most of a hard life amid strong temptation. Even among the adults whom I thus visited, I had seen a growing improvement, especially in their watching and striving against such mere animal impulses as are certain to lead to sensual gratification. There were also evident signs of striving after that which is good, for some had been enabled to look to Jesus as their Saviour. On the part of the children I could see a marked change for the better. An incident occurred sometime after which led me to know that this was not a vain hope. One of the houses which I had then described as dangerous to the inmates as well as unfit for human habitation, fell, and life was lost. A boy, who thereby passed into eternity, was able to rejoice in Jesus, and that boy was one of my best scholars. For the moment I felt as if I could remain; but not having enough to support my own at home, I felt also that I could no longer resist the invitation to labour elsewhere."

And in him " the friendly feeling" became more intense, as if taking possession of him for the first time. He " felt them as if they had suddenly grown up in all their beauty and freshness." He says : " By this time my real friends were few compared with the professed friends I once had; but those on whom I could not count had been tested, while others, as cordial, had proved their sincerity—some in wise, wise words of deep sympathy, others in loving deeds. In some of the more genial and hearty instances—such as in the case of Alexander Smith, the poet—the pleasant and elevating comingling of soul was mutually ardent. Hence it was that my farewell visit to such dear friends, Professor Blackie and others, was very trying to me."

" TRAIN TO LONDON"—A PATRIOTIC DREAM.

"'Take seats. Train for London,' said the guard at the Waverley Station, Edinburgh, on a Friday night, the 14th of

December, 1860. I obeyed, and in a few minutes more the train started. The night was dark and cold, but I was too excited to notice the one or feel the other. Some of my fellow-passengers made way for sleep, and some took to reading; but I was not in a mood for either, so I began to think, in dreamy mood, while the train swept by station after station, only stopping at a few. Various were the themes that claimed consideration, and at last the conviction that our merciful Father was ever near gave point to my thoughts. I could not enter on the question, Why has all this been? I could look at results, and praise God that He had made the 'all things' work together for good. I felt sure that the preparation for the work on which I hoped to enter was severe, but it was a *preparation*, and that was something; and then the severity might yet help some poor one to realize the truth in the phrase, 'A fellow feeling makes us wondrous kind.'

"In course of time such thoughts of God allayed the excitement which accompanied me into the train; and though I could not sleep, my mind settled down to something like a dream. 'Old Caledonia' and many of her doings came before me in a manner very distinct. This seemed very natural, for though I could not but look upon her as 'stern and wild,' yet I could not help regarding her as a 'meet nurse' for a struggling as well as a 'poetic child.' As I thought of her own rugged history—she, too, said I to myself; yes, she, too—during her times of trial and preparation—had her life struggles; and these very struggles stirred in her that daring which led on to that enterprize that has resulted in the attainment of her present position in the United Kingdom—in the world. The volumes which in other days I had devoured, now unfolded page after page of the history of the

'Land of brown heath and shaggy wood.'

Not merely the stirring events of the more romantic days of

early life—days of dun shields and gleamy spears, when the voice of her warriors rang through the echoing isles like the thunder of heaven, when her stately sons were fleet as the roe and brave as the lion. These were thrilling times; but I thought more of her peaceful days—of the glorious triumphs of persevering industry, requiring a zeal as warm, a heroism as daring, an energy as hardy—towering to the utmost heights of knowledge and honour by study and effort, constant labour and effective skill—meeting the contingencies of life and the vicissitudes of a society in which civilisation in the highest and best sense is evident and active—proving her stamina and endurance by a wise and persevering application of her self-made opportunities.

"And then I had also not unfrequently felt those emotions that spring into being and seldom die, when, on her towering mountains gloomy night had spread her darkest mantle, and the vivid lightning darted along as on the wings of the wind—when the hoarse moan of the hoary cliffs had been replied to by the sullen roar of the distant stream, dashing in its foamy course from crag to crag. In sunny days, too, I had traversed her lonely dales and sequestered shades, by the side of her placid lakes and crystal streamlets—through her green woods and leafy bowers—watching the flight of the lark or listening to the song of the blackbird—admiring the shaggy thistle or the wild daisy.

"These days and contemplations—the sounds that seemed even yet to rush into my ears, and the sights that even now flashed before my eyes—were not without their fruit. All this and much more—such as the poets and the poetry of Scotland —led me mentally to exclaim:—

> 'Land of my sires! what mortal hand
> Can e'er untie the filial band
> That knits me to thy rugged strand.'

And after a little more musing, this 'land of the mountain and the flood' rose up before me in all her grandeur and beauty, and then came the other question:—

> 'Breathes there a man with soul so dead,
> Who never to himself hath said,
> This is my own, my native land?'

Verily, I felt I was not the man."

ANOTHER "TRAIN"—OF THOUGHT—ON THE LINE.

"'Tickets for London,' said a railway servant who was accompanied by the guard, and who kindly helped me into the carriage at Waverley Station. His kind inquiries showed he had taken some interest in me—perhaps he had noticed the parting at that station as he called out 'Be seated,' or perhaps he thought I was a poor passenger for such a journey, for I was yet somewhat weak and very pale, so he said.

"'Perhaps this is your first journey to the great city?' said the guard, inquiringly, and left abruptly, for the time to start was come."

This was enough. Our exhausted friend had become even more than usually sensitive. Every word was suggestive, every sentence must become the subject of consideration. And so it was with what fell from the lips of this attentive guard. "Yes," added the weary traveller to himself, "this is my first journey to the great city, and what shall be my lot?"

This question went deep down, and something like a sigh of sadness came, accompanied by some tears. "I ought to have been stronger in God," he added, after a pause. "He had so preserved me and mine that my answer should have been—

> 'He *will* sustain my weakest powers
>   With His almighty arm,
> And watch my most unguarded hours
>   Against surprising harm.'

But then we are so weak when, in being tested, we look to ourselves instead of running to the Refuge. "Going to London," he added, still mentally, and then followed the questions—"How many have gone to this great city to push their way through life? How many to sink? How many to rise? How many to leave the paths of righteousness? How many to walk closer with God? I had known some who had gone to London to endure drudgery, to live in poverty, to regret they had left home—some who, after manifesting courage, had yielded in despair and died in obscurity, unlamented as well as unknown. But then I had also heard of others who had entered the mighty metropolis to observe and inquire, to wait the proper time, to take the proper place in that great whirlpool of life; others, too, who had become useful and respected, favourable circumstances—coupled with industry, frugality, perseverance, and sagacity—bringing pecuniary resources and well-bought honours. And, as I thought again, I asked the question—What shall be my lot?"

THE GREAT CITY.

Truly there is something thrilling in this question, put to himself while within a few miles of the Great City, as it is properly characterised. Sometime after writing on "Arriving in London," he expressed the extremes of the diversity of feeling with which that great centre is entered, when he exclaimed, "How different must have been the impression made on the mind of the Princess Alexandra when passing through London for the first time as the Princess of Wales, from that of a deserted penniless woman from the country in search of her cruel, faithless husband."

Certainly this is the gold and the copper side of the shield over again; but it is only one of the thousands of reflections which have been written about people entering the mighty city for the first time. Whatever may be the condition, if there is the ability to reflect, generally the first feeling is usually that of vague wonder, tinctured with terror, somewhat as we could conceive a tiny stream, were it conscious, feeling when joining the ocean—or of that of a spirit entering the capital of the universe. In coming into this great Babylon, one is first struck with the vast size of the place, with the image it presents of immensity, then the bustle in its streets, the eager haste and hurrying in from all quarters towards that stupendous pile of gloom through which no eye can penetrate, and then with the increasing sound like enginery of an earthquake at work, rolling from the heart of that profound and indefinable obscurity, while sometimes a faint and yellow beam of the sun strikes here and there on the vast expanse of edifices, and (in the fine thought of Burke when he entered the metropolis) churches and holy asylums are dimly seen lifting up their countless steeples and spires, like so many lightning-rods to avert the wrath of Heaven.

The inhabitants resemble ants in an enormous anthill when it is disturbed, and blackens, and they seem less moving at their own individual will than under the pressure of some imperious destiny, some inscrutable purpose, of which they are the mere puppets and playthings.

Then there follows a sense of unutterable insignificance, a feeling so overpowering and humiliating at first that one is tempted to commit some crime or perpetrate some absurdity, in order to attract attention amid that sea of strange faces and forms which is sweeping carelessly, ceaselessly, callously by.

And all this suppose you are independent of London, and have got your bread elsewhere. But let the man be entering poor and in search of employment, or unknown and craving for fame, he will regard the city, with its dome of St Paul's, as a great, grim, black idol, which he must, in some way and by some enchantment, propitiate, or else be plucked into its burning arms and consumed to ashes.

Or, when the mind has leisure or inclination to turn from

its own concerns to a general review of the city, what thoughts arise! Doubtless they are elevating and inspiring, as it revolves the many majestic movements to which London is the centre —the commerce, the literature, the art, the benevolent enterprise, the political action, the moral and spiritual influence, the whole nations of important and able men it contains within its limits, the noble buildings, institutions, and churches it folds within its ample arms—the ever-playing pulse of active, useful life which beats within its veins. But, alas! close under these glorious thoughts there lurk the giant shadows, poverty, guilt, vice, fraud, folly, misery, madness, soundless abysses of sin and woe—the murder-alleys, theft-corners, lust-lanes, and broad blasphemy squares of this City of destruction—the gin-palaces, brothels, gambling-houses, the whole streets of starvation, the thousand and one underground railways to hell, and rivers of loud-sounding or lazy perdition.

To feel that one is amongst this, or a portion of it, or separated from it only by a bed-chamber wall,—there is something very sublime but most appalling in the conception, and one lying down at night feels as if resting on the thin edgeway between the celestial city and pandemonium—the groans and ghastly imprecations of the one mingling with and overpowering the songs and symphonies of the other.

And this was the city into which Mr Hillocks entered on a foggy December morning, 1860; not acquainted with its grandeur, or terror, or mystery, but eager to enter the noble army there manfully fighting against the myriad-armed demon who had, as he still has, such an empire within. Into this "broad field of battle" our friend was anxious to enter, to "be a hero in the strife," "still achieving still pursuing," as one among the thousands of humble, useful men—ready for any amount of self-denial and self-sacrifice, if only they, by God's help, might assist in making London better, lessening its sins and sorrows, promoting its purity and happiness.

CHAPTER XVIII.

THE *RESUMÉ*—FROM DECEMBER, 1860.

HAVING thus traced our friend's earlier struggles—his career from the cradle to London—there is a natural tendency to run on even to his latest successes; but that cannot be done at present, at least, in detail. To give a fair outline of his Life and Work since 1860, would require another volume as large as this one. Therefore, all that can be added here is a brief *resumé* from that date to the present. But even this will show that the child is father to the man—that the work of preparation in Scotland has not been lost. Still he can say as he has often said—

"The Lord that built the earth and sky is my perpetual aid."

This may be seen to some extent in his volume entitled "Mission Life in London;"* but as only a few copies of that work remain, we shall avail ourselves of a brief narrative drawn up by a friend. This, we understand, is selected from various sources, such as the sketch which appeared in the "Northern Light," and a later sketch which appeared after the railway collision in which he was so severely injured. These brief notes are classified according to their date, and the first series refer to

* Hodder and Stoughton, London.

HIS FIRST TWO YEARS IN LONDON.

In the volume just named, Mr Hillocks says—" The Rev. J. H. Wilson received me kindly on my arrival at his office, then in Bloomfield-street, E.C. But he very properly thought I was too weak to preach on the morrow, so I rested on the Sunday. It turned out, however, in the course of the week, that I was once more to realise the meaning of the sentence— "There is much between the cup and the lip;" but in this case the cause sprung from a slight mistake, but no blame anywhere. Mr Wilson's letter, containing the invitation, was sent through his Edinburgh friend, who, on reading it, and seeing the words *this week*, wrote to London to say he feared I could not be there so early as to be able to preach on the Sunday. This letter of invitation came to me, and not knowing that any letter had been sent in reply, I wrote to say I might be expected in time. But before my note arrived Mr Wilson had written for another preacher, to prevent any disappointment. The result was, the people liked the man and he remained with them.

"I need not say this was a disappointment to me, to my family and friends. Mr Wilson assured me that there might be another opening ere long; but here I was in London, and almost without a penny. Something must be done immediately, so I became 'a man of business' once more—having made a temporary engagement with Mr Tweedie, the publisher, who was then in the act of bringing out the Second Edition of 'Life Story.'

"This was a first-rate school, and I learned much. I was an odd man, but not in an odd place—in almost every place and at everything—now supplying the world with temperance literature, now assisting on the A B C Railway Guide, now correcting proof paragraphs—news and other correspondence sent to the *Temperance Record;* now writing reviews and articles for it. Then came the evening lectures, all *gratis*. I was sought for everywhere for the temperance and other meetings—from Surrey Chapel in the South, to the Cabinet Theatre in the North—from the West to the East.

"I say from the West, for soon after I arrived in London I was introduced to the authoress of 'Ragged Homes and How to Mend Them,' who was at that time doing good work in the Potteries. There, in connection with this work, I met the Rev. Henry Varley for the first time. There, too, I met my countryman, the Rev. Dr Tait, now the Archbishop of Canterbury. It was at one of these meetings, chiefly composed of the gipsies, that I stole a march on the bishop. We were both to address the meeting—he first, of course. The address was very good, but the people seemed to listen because the speaker was a bishop. I happened to be a little more successful, for the audience applauded frequently. 'Is he a missionary among the gipsies?' asked Dr Tait. The secret was this: After taking a cup of tea hastily at the platform table, I went down among the people; talked with one and another, especially among the younger portion of them. I told them some things about Scotland, and they told me much about the Potteries, their life and ways of living. I caught their words and some of their phrases. This, with the newly-acquired knowledge, enabled me to make several points, I hope for good.

"I was not long in London when I felt it was my duty to know more of the English people before undertaking the responsibilities of a pastorate. This I told the friends who were the means of my coming to the metropolis, suggesting, too, that I would rather be an evangelist for a time. So I continued the clerk, the sub, the reviewer, the lecturer, occasionally supplying vacant pulpits, until Mr Wilson received a letter containing this question—'Could not Mr Hillocks' services be retained for North London?' My friends agreed, and I was willing. The 'services' were clustered under two heads—that of the missionary and the lecturer."

HIS NEW SPHERE AND ACTION.

These faculties did not manifest themselves so fully nor so powerfully in his Islington sphere as they afterwards did in his next field of labour, in St Pancras, where he commenced that course of heroic self-denying efforts which endeared him to the poor.

"There were," he says, "some ladies and gentlemen connected with my work at Islington for whom I have ever retained feelings of respect and gratitude. Their help and encouragement in the work were cheering and valuable, but the happy results of all this were greatly marred by the narrow views and sectarian spirit of others. Among the Christian workers of St Pancras, or rather among those who invited me there, there was less of the unfavourable element. 'Do what you can, in the best way you can,' are words which convey the spirit of the agreement upon which I entered this wide field of labour."

He went there as an Evangelist under the auspices of the London Congregational Association, and the junction of the Hampstead and Tottenham Court Roads, Euston Road, was regarded as the centre of action—the circumference being left very much to circumstances and his judgment. Near to this is Tolmer's Square Congregational Church, with the learned pastor of which Mr Hillocks was closely and happily associated. Though now separated by the Tweed, Mr Hillocks speaks of "this beloved friend in the best of bonds" as "a Christian in the highest style of man," as "hearty and genial, liberal and loving." Each attended to his own department of Christian duty, and each helped the other.

But apart from such, his fellow-workers in this rather wide vineyard, Mr Hillocks found much that was neither pleasant to see nor to hear. Of the physical aspect, he says:—"At first sight—when passing through the leading thoroughfares of this expansive district—the general aspect seemed somewhat favourable; but a glance at the smaller streets, courts, and places soon led to the conviction that things were not what they seemed. There were numerous parts densely peopled, and generally they were as dirty as they were narrow, in many cases very filthy."

Of the "moral waste," he adds:—"There was a greater variety in the population of St Pancras than in Islington; and, alas, the spectacles of guilt and misery were even more visible and hideous in the former than the latter—the brand of the devil standing out in bolder relief. But God enabled me to do good here, too, among those who had been besmeared in the filthy mires of the moral marshes, not a few having blindly plunged into deep wretchedness, while others were rushing impetuously to sad destruction."

To raise such, by divine help, "to God and usefulness," he set to work most heartily, and, as we see, very successfully. In the report of the London Congregational Association, February 25, 1864, we read:—"The mission under Mr Hillocks in the north-western district has been abundantly blessed. He has opened for himself and his Gospel message a door into many hearts. We find he is doing much, under God, to link the poor to the new sanctuary, and we feel it would be a calamity to lose his services."

To tell how, and by what means, God enabled him to open the door to the people's heart would occupy a large portion of a volume; but the following sentence may give an indication. He says:—"In addition to visiting the people at their homes, indoor and outdoor services, popular lectures, and many kindred efforts—often speaking sixteen times a week to large audiences—I had to go to plead at the police courts, attend the sick at the hospitals, and help the poor at the workhouses."

In the course of time, and step by step, his organising abilities came out to advantage, in the formation of the

Christian Instruction, the Total Abstinence, the Mending Home, the Mutual Benefit, and other Societies—all united and working under the general name of the North-west London Evangelistic Association, of which Samuel Morley, M.P., was the president. There was also a Juvenile Department of this work, having children's services, a Band of Hope, the Provident, and other such bands.

Thus the work went on and enlarged year by year, into the details of which we cannot enter here, simply selecting one of the leading incidents of his Mission Life in that parish, showing the width of the meaning he applied to the injunction, "Do the work of an evangelist"—taking in the full view of that passage, and extending it to the care and protection of the helpless poor.

BATTLING FOR THE POOR—WORKHOUSE HORRORS.

He was a frequent visitor at St Pancras' Workhouse, always made welcome in "the wards," but dreaded at "the board-room." At this time, in almost every London workhouse, but especially in the parish in which Mr Hillocks' lot had been cast, parochial matters were such as to be far from being favourable to the honest poor. This was soon evident to him, and he at once felt it his duty to help such as far as possible, to the "annoyance" of those of the heartless "in authority," the so-called Guardians. He says:—" Their inhumanity had gone beyond belief, and had it not been for the terrible fact daily brought before me, I would have regarded it as beyond conception. And, alas, I had reason to fear that, with a few rare instances, public feeling, in regard to private suffering, was almost dead. There were here and there some noble exceptions in St Pancras. Even at the parochial board, all were not so heartless; but, as a body, it was remorseless in its horrid cruelty and shameless in its neglect; as daring, too, as if there were no Christian hearts in the parish. I could not go with the stream, and I suffered for it. Finding they were almost as heedless as they were heartless, I tried the pen as well as the tongue, and the Press readily seconded my efforts. But the case of 'the child laid out alive,' brought matters to a crisis. I found 'poor wee Bessie Green' in the children's ward, prepared for the deadhouse while still alive. This led to a renewed battle, which lasted for nearly two years. I felt so horrified that I wrote to the Poor Law Board, describing the scene, and pleading for their immediate inquiry into the case. Though sorely tempted, I carefully avoided all exasperation of utterance. I felt sure that the simple statement of the fearful facts was enough to touch the hearts of all having in them the least spark of humanity. And I was right; the bare narrative made the nation shudder, and roused the indignation of London. On the day after my letter appeared, first in the *Times*, one of the many newspapers which, in a leader, took up the case, wrote—'Of all the workhouse horrors that have yet been shown there is none more harrowing than that narrated by the Rev. J. I. Hillocks.' And a city gentleman, writing to me in my affliction—after the battle was fought and the victory won—and referring to the letter, said, 'Your writing direct to the Poor Law Board was a God-inspired act on behalf of the suffering and helpless poor.'"

According to the evidence of the nurse and others in the workhouse, the child died a few hours after. Mr Hillocks demanded that the dead clothes be loosed; hence Dr Lancaster, the coroner, held an inquest upon the baby body. And the evidence given by Mr Hillocks, and even by the workhouse officials, added horror to horror. The *Lancet*, having carefully and skilfully watched the case throughout, said: "The verdict of the coroner's jury may be regarded with unqualified satisfaction. It is the verdict of the ratepayers of the parish, delivered without a charge from the coroner, on the evidence upon oath of the officers of the workhouse."

The verdict was that the death of the child was greatly accelerated by being laid out for dead, while alive, swaddled like a corpse. And to their verdict they appended three special resolutions, namely:—

"The jury are of opinion that great blame is to be attributed to the workhouse attendants for tying up the jaws of the deceased and treating her as dead for some time before she had expired.

"That they are further of opinion that there is not a sufficient number of paid medical attendants and nurses to perform the duties of so large an establishment as St Pancras workhouse.

"And the jury beg to express their approval of the course taken by Mr Hillocks in bringing the matter before the public."

The Poor Law Board also appointed their Commissioner to open an inquiry into the case, giving him power to take the evidence on oath. And the decision of the Poor Law Board was the same in substance as the verdict and resolutions of the Jury. But all this—the shame and censure—would have been easily pocketed by the authorities of St Pancras, had it not been the third resolution. This was the sting that made them kick, and they did kick. But this only made matters worse for them in the end, and better for the poor. "*Their* cause," says Mr Hillocks, "was bad; *mine* was good. Their denials led to more revelations, and at last they thought of gaining a point by trying hard to find a flaw in my moral character; and failing that, they, as they thought, found a mare's nest in the undeniable fact that I was *once a weaver*. This was proclaimed on the house-top; and on one grand occasion the question was most pompously put—'Is this vast parish, wielding so much money annually, to be governed by a Dundee Weaver?'"

The Baroness Burdett-Coutts addressed the "Guardians"

in language befitting the occasion, and bespeaking her well-known sympathy for the suffering poor, closed her letter thus: "Against such a system of administration, which actually exposes paupers to the danger of being buried alive, I must enter my protest; and that not only on my own account as a ratepayer, but also on behalf of that large and struggling body of ratepayers upon whom the maintenance of the workhouse presses heavily."

But all in vain; she, too—as well as the Archbishop of York—was bullied to silence, and Mr Hillocks was once more left single-handed in the struggle, save an occasional help from the papers. One closed a powerful article with these words:— "Even those disbelievers in the sanctity of St Pancras will find it hard to say who are responsible for acts that look like so many outrages on humanity. Of course, if everybody were like Mr Hillocks, things might be different; but, then, it is the fashion now-a-days to say that religious philanthropists of his stamp are actuated by base motives; and, indeed, we are afraid that the Hillockses of this world are out of harmony with the 'admirable system of pauper protection' established in our metropolitan workhouses."

In time, however, the Government took up the matter in earnest. To prevent a repetition of such horrid cruelties, an Act of Parliament was passed as quickly as possible, and applied to St Pancras'. Soon after it became law, it not only turned all those in authority right about, but made it much more difficult for such enemies of the poor to regain place and power.

CHILDREN'S DINNERS—LEAVING FOR THE COUNTRY.

But this defence of the helpless, leading to triumph, was not the only way in which Mr Hillocks sought to relieve the suffering poor. Another was giving dinners to the starving children. He thus gives the origin of this now widely-spread Institution :—" Ever after reading of Victor Hugo's Christmas Dinners for Poor Children, the thought that what was good for Christmas time might be useful on other days kept close to me. There had also been established by some kind friends, what was called the Invalid Children's Table, at which some sickly children had dinner occasionally ; and these friends, at times, assisted one or two starving children, for whom I pleaded; but what was that among so many ? I brought the matter before my Young Samaritan Society, and asked their help to try to be able to give a wholesome dinner to a thousand poor children that winter. The better-to-do of this noble Band— led by my own son and his sisters—rendered great help ; and even some of its poorest members gave considerable assistance."

This work went on extending, help coming from various sources and in various forms. During this conflict, chiefly in the winters, 3,207 hearty and healthy dinners were given in his own house, besides what were sent to those too weakly or sickly to come for them. And not a few boys and girls were clothed, and otherwise prepared for service and situations. " It is pleasant," he says, " to think that nearly all who were thus protected and provided for have proved themselves worthy of the efforts made on their behalf. Wherever I meet them, in England or Scotland, they refer to these days with grateful joy."

But, as might be expected, by the end of this severe struggle, and his triumph over Bumbledom, as Dickens called those in authority in the celebrated Parish of St Pancras, Mr and Mrs Hillocks and children were greatly exhausted, and their days of usefulness were fast closing in this district. On the day after a meeting of rejoicing over the successes which God enabled them to gain over the enemies of the poor, he, in this exhausted state of body and mind, visited a poor family in one of the fever dens, and became a prey to infection, and the next day he was laid down. He was soon dangerously ill. But in course of time God so blessed kind nursing and medical skill, that he rallied so as to give hopes of his complete recovery.

After he was sufficiently strong to withstand the fatigue of travelling, he went to Scotland, frequently breaking his journey, till he went to Tain. The changes of air and the kind treatment of loving friends did so much for him, that in six weeks he returned home, ready for work—so he thought, but was mistaken. Soon after this, a memorial, signed by 254 adults, was presented to him, asking that he become the Pastor of an Evangelistic Church which they proposed to form. He consented, and a committee was appointed—composed of ministers and others—to seek for a suitable site for the building, and otherwise promote the object in view. But during this time it became too evident that he had resumed work too soon after such an illness. By the advice of the doctors and other friends who learned of the serious nature of the relapse, he resigned the duties he had so recently undertaken.

Again he rallied; but change of air, with comparative rest for a longer season, being imperative, his friends were one in the advice that he should go to the country until he became completely restored. Still, even after receiving a unanimous call to become one of the Ministers of the Union-street Congregational Church, Darlington, he felt reluctant to leave those among whom he had laboured for nearly six years. His friends urged the acceptance of this invitation, as the likely means of fully regaining his energy and prolonging his usefulness. The Rev. J. H. Wilson—who knew the whole of the circumstances, as well as the nature and extent of the work under the pressure of which he had to yield—wrote to Mr Hillocks:— "We can ill afford to lose you; for London, with all its sins and sorrows, has a first claim on the best talent and most earnest piety in the land; but, under the circumstances, I should say go, and, if you come back, you shall soon find another sphere in London."

Among other letters of advice was one from the Rev. Dr Guthrie, of Edinburgh. He said—"My dear Friend, I know what such city work as yours is. I had years of it, and it is a burden both on mind and body—a strain on the nervous system greater than one can stand beyond a certain limit. However, your London experience, as well as your training in Scotland, will prove of the greatest value, especially with your natural aptitude for the work of the pulpit and ministry. You know how much I have esteemed you. I think the people will be favoured who enjoy your services."

He, at last, accepted the call; but before he left for his new sphere of labours, the friends cheered and assisted him, as is seen in the following paragraph from one of the newspapers of that date, April, 1868:—

"PRESENTATION.—At a public meeting held a few weeks ago, it was unanimously resolved to present a testimonial to the Rev. J. I. Hillocks, on his retirement from his labours here through severe illness. A committee was appointed to carry out that object. On Tuesday evening a deputation waited on Mr Hillocks at his residence, Delancey-street, and there they presented to him the testimonial. It consisted of a purse of money and an elegantly bound quarto volume, entitled 'The Bible Album; or, Sacred Truth illustrated by the Poets.' The following inscription was inserted in the book—'Presented to the Rev. James Inches Hillocks and Mrs Hillocks, with a purse of money, as a token of hearty appreciation of their self-sacrificing, unsectarian, and useful labours in the cause of Christ— in the physical, educational, and spiritual welfare of the masses —especially the suffering poor in and round that district, the centre of which is the converging portions of Hampstead, Euston, and Tottenham court Roads. This mark of affectionate regard was presented on the occasion of Mr Hillocks resigning his duties here—because of failing health through over-exertion in his arduous labours—by Christian friends, and those who have been benefited by his ministrations. This joint offering is accompanied with the earnest prayer that he may be soon completely restored to health and usefulness, and that the God of love and peace may be with him and his family wherever they may be called to labour."

Alexander Bremner, Esq., one of the first of Mr Hillocks' many co-workers in this district, and one of the Deacons of Tolmer's-square Church, presented this testimonial in a short, warm, and touching speech. Mr Hillocks, in a few appropriate words, expressed his gratitude and that of his family for the marks of Christian sympathy bestowed by warm and constant friends, especially in the times of trial. Other friends took part in the meeting, expressing their joy that Mrs Hillocks' name was connected with the testimonial—she having done so much not only to encourage and help her husband, but also done so much in feeding the poor and helpless in her own house. The proceedings terminated with prayer on behalf of Mr Hillocks and the family."

The following extract from Mr Bremner's letter contains the substance of his address on this occasion. Being a co-worker, he well knew what Mr Hillocks had done and endured. Therefore, this note is the more valuable, given here as a befitting close of an interesting period of the Evangelist's noble and useful career in this district. In that letter, addressed to Mr Hillocks a few days before the presentation of this testimonial, Mr Bremner says:—"Though your health has been impaired, yet when I know that you have been often called even from your bed to assist the outcast to shelter and food—thus labouring in season and out of season, with energy and courage—it is a matter of surprise and gratitude that your strength was so long equal to the trying occasion. And when

I take into account the extent of the sphere of action, the difficulties you have had to fight against in defending the helpless, relieving the destitute, and directing the wanderer, I feel sure there are very few who could have accomplished so much as you have been enabled to do. You have thus certainly added greatly to your knowledge of human life and character in their varied forms, and have, I trust, become more and more fitted for increased usefulness in the Christian Church, both for the Pastoral and Evangelistic work."

CHAPTER XIX.

THE *RESUMÉ* CONTINUED.

TWO YEARS IN THE COUNTRY.

IT was early in May, 1868, he entered upon his duties at Darlington. The season was favourable, and being removed from the suffering and sadness which encircled him in London, he soon revived, and became as active as ever.

Through the kindness of the Right Hon. Lord Kinnaird, he was introduced to the late Joseph Pease, and hence to the other members of that worthy family, who greatly and kindly encouraged him in the special work for which he soon became known—for the social as well as the religious improvement of the people.

As soon as his health permitted, he accepted of the invitation to take his place at the Cottage Hospital in the order of attendance with the other ministers of the town. He was also elected a member of the Darlington Ministerial Association, which met monthly for prayer and mutual edification. In April his name was also added to the list of ministers of the Congregational Evangelistic Union of South-west Durham. His coming to Darlington, as well as the progress of his work there, was noticed in very appreciative tones by the newspapers and magazines of the district. A short sketch of his life and work, up to his coming to Darlington, appeared in the *Northern Light*, a Congregational monthly. It was, we understand, from the able pen of the Rev. H. T. Robjohns, then of Newcastle.

As was understood, Mr Hillocks' department of the work was chiefly to take the oversight of the surrounding preaching stations, but more especially to work up the one in the north-end of the town, with the view of forming it into a distinct church. This he accomplished in little more than a year, at which time he resigned the co-pastorate to take full charge of the north-end congregation. The July number of the *Northern Light*, 1869, thus records this event: "On Thursday, June 3rd, was formed what is to be known as the North-end Congregational Church. The members elected Mr Hillocks as their pastor."

But fuller notices appeared in other publications. The *Darlington Telegraph*, for instance, in the course of a long report, says:—"As our readers are aware, about a year ago (May, 1868), the Rev. J. I. Hillocks came from London. Since that time he has laboured successfully in our midst. Ultimately it was perceived that it would be for the greater good if his efforts were confined chiefly to the north-end of our town, where there is a large population of ironworkers and others in want of the help which he, as a minister and social reformer, is able and anxious to render. This step in the right direction was taken on Thursday by the formation of what is now known as the North-end Congregational Church, at a special meeting held at the usual place of worship, Albert Road. The Rev. H. Kendall, and other office-bearers of Union Street Church, were present to bid God speed to the new cause. After the devotional exercises, conducted by Mr Hillocks, Mr Kendall was requested to take the chair. In doing so, he stated that it gave him great pleasure to be present and to congratulate Mr Hillocks and those friends who had worked so earnestly with him in the north-end. Resolutions in relation to the formation of this new church were adopted, and after the singing of a suitable hymn, Mr Kendall read the call which had been unanimously adopted by that church, inviting Mr Hillocks to become its pastor. To this hearty invitation Mr Hillocks gave a ready consent, and stated that with God's help he would, to the utmost of his ability, and to the full extent of his opportunity, attend to the feeding of the flock, to the advancement of the congregation in knowledge and usefulness, and to the prosperity of the Sabbath school; never for a day losing sight of the surrounding mission field, knowing that those who had already laboured with him in it would continue their efforts with increasing faith and energy. The meeting was afterwards addressed by Mr Kendall and others in words expressing wise counsel and kindly sympathy, as well as fraternal greeting towards pastor and people. Most cordially do we join in wishing that Mr Hillocks and his people may prosper, not only as a church and congregation, but also in the various useful movements with which his name is associated, and upon which he bestows much thought and effort for the general good."

The progress of this church under his care is indicated by a notice of one of its social meetings six months after. The *Darlington Mercury*, in its usual local intelligence, recording this tea meeting, said:—"The chair was occupied by Mr Hillocks, the Pastor, who, in his opening address, complimented the office-bearers, teachers, and other workers on their earnestness, unity, and effort. The Rev. H. Kendall also addressed the meeting, adding that the success which had attended this cause was to him a source of great pleasure. A church, like man, required years to grow to maturity. Great care, as well as much effort, were needed, but they had already proved what a noble purpose, with common sense and God's help, can do. The Rev. H. Phillips then delivered an excellent address on Christian duty, having special reference to labours connected with the building up of a cause and its extension. He was glad to learn what had been done, but he knew Mr Hillocks would not be content with that. Mr Hillocks was just the man to assign each worker a proper place and keep all at work."

Nor was he less successful in what might be called his "outside work," especially that department of it on behalf of the children. The *Darlington Telegraph*, in noticing one of the special meetings, at which ex-Mayor Henry Pease presided, and at which almost all the ministers of the town were present, stated that the Rev. H. Phillips moved the first resolution, namely :—" That the Bud of Promise is truly deserving of the practical sympathy of parents and all interested in the temporal, educational, and moral welfare of the young." In supporting this resolution, he said he wished to couple the name of Mr Hillocks with it as the founder and the superintendent of this great and useful work. He was sure, from what he had himself seen, and from all they now saw, that Mr Hillocks and his co-workers in this labour of love deserved the good wishes and the necessary help from all classes and all sects—the movement being quite unsectarian.

In acknowledging a hearty vote of thanks for his disinterested and valuable labours, Mr Hillocks said he could not take all the praise to himself. There was God first, and then the earnest helpers. The *Darlington Mercury*, in its notice, gives an insight into this work. It said—" Though Mr Hillocks came to Darlington to regain health, yet he rested not a day. While ever ready to co-operate heartily with other workers, he struck out new paths for himself. One of these we find in what he has called the Bud of Promise. This juvenile association is composed of boys and girls from six to sixteen years of age. It has in it several bands. Each band has a distinct aim, but all variously tending to the promotion of the common object—namely, the spread of Christian and general knowledge, and the cultivating of industrial and provident habits chiefly among the young."

The *Northern Light* for May, 1870, contained the following

notice:—"The Rev. J. I. Hillocks has resigned the pastorate of Northend Congregational Church, Darlington, after a ministry of two years." He was able to rejoice in past usefulness, regained health, and the formation of new friendships.

Some of his friends, while regretting this separation, quietly but heartily presented Mr Hillocks with a tangible token of their warm attachment; and this, he says, assisted him the better again to enter the great metropolis.

IN THE RAILWAY COLLISION AT HARROW.

Finding himself thoroughly reinvigorated, he returned to London with the view of again enlarging his field of usefulness, and for a time all went well. "My plan," he says, "was to wait the opening of a church wherein I might get full vent to the evangelistic turn of my mind, as well as the opportunity of feeding the flock. To this end I gave myself to supplying vacant pulpits, to lecturing, and organising good work."

A London newspaper, referring to this time, said—"Our readers will be glad to learn that the well-known author of 'Life Story' has returned to London. While waiting the opening of a suitable church, he is doing that for which he is sure to be remembered affectionately by thousands after he has long gone to glory. This, the organizing of work, as well as uniting the workers, seems to be comparatively easy to him, yet it must be a severe strain on body and mind to put forth all his energies, mental and physical, wherever he goes; but it is evident that this is one of the best ways by which he can serve the Church and benefit the world, and hence we hope that churches and societies, and individual philanthropists, may avail themselves of his valuable services before he again resumes the responsibilities of another pastorate."

This was kindly, but while many such good wishes were being expressed, while engagements were coming in upon him, and a course of prosperity was opening before him, affliction and calamity followed each other in rapid succession. On the 16th of September of the same year, his only son, and the first-born, died—a promising student of 17 years of age. And then, only about two months after, on the 26th of November, he was overtaken in one of the most terrific railway collisions which marked that year—1870.

It was Saturday evening, and he was on his way to preach two special evangelistic sermons at Atherstone. From one of the sketches of his life written some time after, we gather these touching sentences:—"How this calamity affected our sorrowing brother is briefly, but touchingly told, in the following note written and issued, on a post card, two days after, by his eldest daughter. In relation to 150 preaching and lecturing and other arrangements—which had been made, or in which he was in the act of making—she said, 'I regret to inform you that dear Papa is one of the sufferers in the serious railway collision at Harrow Station, on Saturday last, and that, consequently he will not be able to carry out the arrangement to be with you as he promised. I am sorry to add, Papa is so seriously injured that he cannot be removed from Harrow.' And, strange enough, on the following day a letter informed the anxious family that the door of a 'suitable' church had opened for him; but Aggie had most reluctantly to reply, 'Papa is so very ill that the doctors and Mamma think it is better that the church do not wait his recovery, which, at present, seems very doubtful. And the doctors believe that, even should he be spared to us, it must be some considerable time before he could undertake the oversight of another church.' It was about three months before he could, with anything like safety, be removed from Harrow to London, even by means of an invalid carriage, and in the care of the nurse and one of the doctors; and for months after he had frequent and severe relapses."

After months of great suffering he so far recovered that it was thought advisable to seek for further restoration in a change of air—to Scotland, of course—where he and the family remained for several months, chiefly at the Melrose Hydropathic Establishment.

"THE CHRISTIAN UNION FOR CHRISTIAN WORK."

Sometime after their return home several deputations waited on him, and many letters were written with the view of having his first utterances on behalf of some good cause. At last, with the leave of the doctors, he promised, conditionally, to preach, and did preach with remarkable freedom and force, to the joy of his medical and other friends, who were afraid as to the result of such an effort.

While others were discussing the possibility of his being able, once more, to undertake the responsibilities of the Pastorate, he, Mrs Hillocks, and the other members of the family, were prayerfully considering another question—For what had God so marvellously spared him? And this question was most carefully canvassed in connection with one which, long before the "accident," had occupied their thoughts, namely—How best to raise the poor to God and usefulness?

This had been his life-thought, especially since he was called to London; and all were of one mind as to God sparing his life in order to help in the solving of this problem. As soon as he was able he went to visit the Rev. Drs Parker and Aveling, James Fleming, Dawson Burns, and other friends who had been associated with him in good work in times past, such as Hugh Owen, Esq. After laying down his plans, and showing the necessity for such work, all wished him God-speed in the undertaking.

He was glad, and thought on—his mind being filled with "the work and how to do it." And, on the evening of the first Sunday in November, 1872, the first meeting of what is now known as The Christian Union *for* Christian Work, was held in his own dining-room. It was a prayer meeting, assembled to ask God's guidance and blessing.

The Lambeth Auxiliary was formed in December of the same year, and the Stoke-Newington Auxiliary in the January following. Mr J. Kerr became President at Lambeth, and E. P. Barton, President at Stoke-Newington. Both proved themselves to be valuable co-workers.

Other fellow-workers rallied round, and some from sources least expected, as the *Christian Standard*, in an article on this Institution, remarked—"Some of those who were once regarded as outcasts are not only brought in, but actually assisting in bringing others under the good influence."

It soon became necessary to look out for suitable premises as central as possible. In the providence of God, Mr Hillocks' attention was drawn to a large empty building in Stoke-Newington Road, by some called the Manor House, by others the College—the latter being the latest purpose for which it had been applied. When first viewed by him, there were about it evident signs of neglect and decay, but there were also the bones (the bricks and stones, and the form) of what had been a grand house. A lease was taken, the necessary alterations made, giving Central Offices, Class and Reading Rooms, and a Hall for our Sunday and week-day Services and Meetings, and becoming the centre of Health and Educational as well as the more strictly Evangelistic Departments. Here, too, were soon established classes for English, Elocution, French, Latin, with the other means of mental, moral, and mutual improvement —assisted by a loan library, and varied occasionally by Instructive Entertainments; the Popular Lectures on Health, History, and Religion, being illustrated by experiments and diagrams.

This is still the centre of operation, and though it was costly to begin with, yet the purpose is so well served that the friends rejoice the effort was made.

The Principles of this Evangelistic, Educational, and Philanthropic Institution have their basis in Faith, Prayer, Love, Work—faith in God and prayer to God, that love to God from which flows love to man, and that work which proves the existence and presence of faith.

The end sought is twofold—health of soul and health of body—that the "whole spirit, soul, and body be preserved blameless unto the coming of our Lord Jesus Christ" (1 Thess. v. 23)—to raise the poor to God and usefulness.

The means employed are varied, according to circumstances or the needs of the case. But, speaking generally, the promotion of the object—saved souls in healthy bodies—is sought for by supplying such missing links in the mission chain as are likely to unite all Christian workers in Christian work, by establishing auxiliaries in every needy corner in London; by encouraging and assisting each auxiliary in its efforts to embrace whatever relates to the wants and well-being of the soul, seeing to the needs and comforts of the body, and otherwise to help the poor to help themselves; having relation to the whole man and the whole duty of man; removing the stumbling blocks out of the way, and using every possible means to human happiness; but more especially and chiefly by preaching the Gospel—presenting a loving Saviour to perishing sinners,—and in connection with this there are systematic visiting, evangelical services, frequent conversations, union conferences, private correspondence, Bible and other classes, public lectures, and special sermons. The correspondence, conferences, lectures, and sermons are not confined to London.

Financial matters, in a work of this kind, call for considerable attention. In this Mr Hillocks is regarded by some of his friends as not having sufficiently weighed the undoubted claims of his family, who are one with him in purpose and effort. The only difficulty which the dear friends whom he consulted saw was the raising of the necessary funds to begin and carry on the work. They told him so, nor was he blind to their reasoning. But he said to himself, God had not only spared his life, but given the means to begin with at least. He referred to the money he had received by way of compensation for the loss he sustained and the suffering he endured because of the railway "accident." He says:—"We (himself and family) did not rush into the work heedlessly, nor did we enter upon it without counting the cost in money and effort. We knew of the proverbial difficulty of gaining attention and securing assistance for a new organization—especially in the midst of so many having a like object—and more especially in relation to one which, while ready to co-operate with all, was bent on finding a special field, rather mode of action, for itself. We also felt assured that, for a time at least, the work we proposed to establish was not likely to be readily countenanced save by those whose views of Christian truth and Christian duty were as liberal as the Gospel in all the fulness of its meaning. Still we felt sure that, if the work was well begun, it would in the end be well supported by those who are really interested in the physical, intellectual, and spiritual welfare of the people. Having the means, we lent it to the Lord with our time and labour, knowing neither would be lost—that all was His."

To this day he is convinced they did right; and, speaking lately on this point, he says:—"Though it were coming to that of it that every door was shut and the whole work to cease, God's blessing on the past overpays all the money that has been spent and all the efforts that have been put forth by us and others in connection with this Institution. I know that my friends have reason on their side when they gently chide me for not being sufficiently careful of my own and my family's comfort. These friends mean well, and I take it all in good part. Looking at the whole matter merely from a human point of view, I have nothing to say; yet I am convinced I did right. And, difficulties not a few, with pressure not easily borne—notwithstanding these—my family agree with me. Whatever sacrifice has been made, the fact that God has been blessing to the joy of saved souls, the delight of inquiring minds, and the comfort of healthier bodies—this fact, with many others of a cheering kind, serves as a strong incentive, and says, 'Go on; look up.'"

At the end of the second year a short appeal for funds was drawn up by the Council, and signed by its Hon. Secretary, and the Hon. Secretary to the Financial Committee. Mr Hillocks agreed to this the more readily because then it was evident the realization was coming up to his expectation. At the end of the third year there were £175 spent more than had been received. This, too, was paid by Mr Hillocks that the work might go on, and because he knew those who had come as helpers were not in any way responsible in money matters. The last paragraph of the appeal runs thus—

"It is our duty also to state here that Mr Hillocks, our General Superintendent, has not, as yet, had any pecuniary remuneration, though from the commencement he has devoted his whole time and energy in the work. His experience and efforts are still necessary to the further development and extension of that work—the commencement of which is one of the happy results of his persevering endeavours as a Christian Worker ever ready to co-operate with all such. But none, save those of independent means, could continue thus to labour without the necessary support—hence we feel confident we have only to mention these facts to secure the help now so much wanted."

This appeal was heartily approved of by the Press—religious, local, and general. The following, from the *Christian World*, may be cited as an example:—"The objects of the Christian Union are to reach and raise people by attention to their temporal and intellectual as well as their spiritual welfare. Many ministerial brethren have expressed their full appreciation of this Christian work, and recommend the appeals for funds to the favourable notice of Christian Philanthropists—a recommendation which we have great pleasure in endorsing."

The results have been incidentally alluded to, and perhaps this is enough here. It may also be stated that there are many circumstances which could not be recorded, they being so closely connected with domestic matters and relatives, yet demanding care, means, and effort from day to day, and, in some cases, lasting for weeks, in the West as well as the East, in the South as well as the North of the great metropolis. It may be stated, too, that though the chief object is to raise the poor, yet there are many kindred aims, and one is to prevent the well-disposed from falling—by fostering all that is good in them, and leading them to be useful helpers in the work. An instance will illustrate. G. W. was one of the first members of the association. He became one of the most successful preachers on the plan, and has just been called to the pastorate of a church in the neighbourhood of London. Writing lately to Mr Hillocks, he says: "I wish most heartily that I could give more assistance to your great work, but I shall not fail to plead for it with all the eloquence I can command, having a practical acquaintance with your noble object and beneficial efforts, to all of which I am a great debtor. It shall ever have my earnest prayers for prosperity, especially when I think of what you have sacrificed to begin the work, and the great weight it must be on your mind, because of the mental and physical labour involved; and above all when I remember that *to that work and yourself I am, under God, indebted for my present position and future prospects.*"

It is a *Home Mission* in the sense that its more immediate influence is confined to London, but already a share of that influence has gone abroad. Some, whose zeal has been increased by kindly encouragement, and who learned and laboured in connection with this work, are now proclaiming the Gospel abroad as Workmen Missionaries.

And while the chief aim and the leading efforts are to win souls and feed them, considerable attention is paid to such means as are likely to be blessed to the alleviation of human suffering, and this under the head of the Health Department. For a time the efforts made in connection with this division of labour were confined chiefly to the use of means likely *to prevent* disease, such as the teaching of the laws of health by lectures, conversations, and readings from the books on the leading subjects; but in time, by the kind and voluntary help of medical men, a consulting staff was formed, and special assistance being given, so that those so pressed by poverty and suffering received all the attention possible, together with home comforts in the Sanatorium—a portion of the establishment set apart for reception of the weak and the weary for rest and restoration.

In all this and other kindred efforts, such as children's dinners and taking food to the homes of the aged and helpless, there is the aim to follow the Healer of men and the Saviour of souls. With Mr Hillocks, Christ is the *only* Saviour and *best* example. And the whole plan of this Institution—developed, and as yet not completely developed—is laid to assist, under God, so that the "whole spirit, soul, and body be preserved blameless unto the coming of our Lord Jesus Christ."

The encouraging notes from dear friends have been of considerable service to him. So early in the history of this work as December, 1872, the Right Hon. Lord Kinnaird wrote:—
"Dear Mr Hillocks—It will give me at all times great pleasure if I can assist in any of the good works you undertake for the

benefit of your fellow-men. It is now many years since I became acquainted with your labours in the cause of our Divine Master, and I rejoice to think that after being laid aside for so long by the fearful accident you met with, you are able in some measure to resume the work on which your heart is set. You have my best wishes for your success."

Another friend—Dr George Johnson, Professor of Medicine, King's College—wrote on Feb. 1873 :—" Dear Mr Hillocks— The Health Department of The Christian Union has for me an especial interest; and I have much pleasure in sending you a small contribution to the funds. As Physician to a large London Hospital, I have had abundant opportunities of learning how much preventable disease among the labouring classes is a direct result of the disregard of obvious sanitary laws. Teach your disciples to acquire habits of cleanliness in their persons and in their dwellings, and to shun alcoholic liquors, and you will diminish to an incalculable degree the demand for hospitals, prisons, and lunatic asylums. I heartily wish you God-speed in the Christian work in which you and your fellow-labourers are engaged."

This work has just entered upon its fifth year, and every lover of all truly Christian efforts for the physical comfort, intellectual improvement, and spiritual advancement of the people will be glad to hear of its continued progress and lasting usefulness. Mr Hillocks closed one of his addresses to his fellow-labourers by saying, " To a great extent, our increasing usefulness depends on our fellowship with Jesus as our best Example as well as the only Saviour—the Healer of men as well as the Saviour of souls—and this by faith and effort— abiding in Him and breaking every yoke—ever remembering that we are sent forth as sheep in the midst of wolves, and must therefore be wise as serpents and harmless as doves. Yes, let us have faith and let us pray, let us have hope and work in love; but we must be wise, daily 'renewed in knowledge'—the knowledge of God, His character and will—of the Gospel, its nature and power—of man, '*spirit, soul, and body*,' the evil that injures him and the good that would heal him. Let us have a clear insight of the Laws from Heaven for Life on Earth. Looking, loving, following Jesus,

> 'Let us *now* be up and doing,
> With a heart for any fate;
> Still achieving, still pursuing,
> Learn to labour and to wait.'"

Works by David Macrae.

THE AMERICANS AT HOME.

OPINIONS OF THE PRESS ON FIRST EDITION.

In reviewing this work the *British Quarterly* says:—"We do not hesitate to aver that in many respects this is the best, as it is certainly the most amusing, book of American delineations we have met with; and it is written with an enthusiasm so genuine, and in a spirit so excellent, that it will be read by Americans with as much pleasure as by Englishmen, and will certainly do much to nourish the best feelings between the two nations."

The *Westminster Review* says:—"Mr. Macrae's 'Pen and Ink Sketches of American Men, Manners, and Institutions,' is a really good work on America, which deserves to be cordially welcomed. It is replete with racy and original anecdotes, abounds with realistic pictures of American life and character, and contains, in many parts, vigorous political reflections and conclusions, which of themselves are sufficient to impart to the work no ordinary value."

The *London Quarterly* says:—"With the instructiveness of a cyclopædia it combines the excitement of a romance. It is the most intelligent, thoroughly sympathetic, and trustworthy account of the Americans we have seen."

The *Saturday Review*, comparing it with the works of Trollope and Dixon, says:—"The one kind of writer on America who seems exceptionally rare is the one who can tell us without prejudice what he has seen. To this class, on the whole, Mr. Macrae belongs."

The Rev. GEO. GILFILLAN says:—"From Mr. Macrae's antecedents we were certain that the book he was to produce on America could not possibly be dull. He has for four or five years been well known as a dashing newspaper writer, as well as the author of that series of clever squibs commencing with 'The Trial of Dr. Norman

Macleod for the Alleged Murder of Mr. Moses Law,' which has increased the gaiety of the Scottish nation, and wreathed a rich arabesque border of laughter around the solemn groundwork of recent ecclesiastical discussions, which, verily, without it would have been dull and stupid enough. Mr. Macrae has a keen eye for the ridiculous; can catch and paint personal characteristics admirably; is good, as some one says of Sydney Smith, or rather as Sydney Smith says of somebody else, 'at abating and dissolving pompous gentlemen;' writes a pointed style; and although he holds very decided opinions on many topics, is candid and courteous to his opponents."

The *London Nonconformist* says:—"If a Scotchman by birth, he is not insular in his sympathies. He understands and realizes the full import of Republican Government; he sees its advantages and its disadvantages; and traces misgovernment and political corruption to their true source. He is fair and even generous towards the American people."

The *Daily Review* says:—"It is the most valuable contribution made in recent years to the library of American travel."

The *Examiner and Review* said, in an article on the subject:—"There is an absence of exaggeration and a truthfulness of detail about these sketches of Mr. Macrae's which make them exceedingly valuable. We know not any book on the social condition and material progress of the United States which we should prefer to the amusing and suggestive volumes before us."

The *American Register* says:—"This elaborate work may fairly be classed among the best productions describing our country and its inhabitants. It is written in a fluent and easy style, brimful of 'photographs of life,' and of interesting anecdotes, such as no description can rival."

The *Petersburg (Virginia) Index* says:—"It is not often that a foreign tourist can gather so many facts, see so much of things and men and manners, observe them in so catholic a spirit, and convey the results of his journey in so pleasing and clear a style."

Putman's (American) Magazine says:—"Mr. Macrae is a good observer, and an impartial judge. He travelled over the whole country, from Canada to New Orleans, not in the beaten routes only, but in out-of-the-way places, and everywhere kept his eyes and ears open, and his heart in the right place."

The *Cosmopolitan*, published in London, Paris, and New York, says:—"The 'Americans at Home' is one of the best and fairest books on the subject that we have seen for years."

THE SOCIAL HYDRA:

OR,

THE INFLUENCE OF THE TRAFFIC OF PAWNBROKERS AND BROKERS ON THE CONDITION OF THE WORKING CLASSES AND THE POOR.

"A lucid, well-arranged, and apparently exhaustive description of a very wasteful and hideous ulcer on the body politic. The disclosures of the pamphlet are perfectly frightful. The author has ransacked police returns, poor-law reports, home-mission records, and every source, as it would appear, whence information was to be obtained. The research he has thus imposed on himself entitles him to the gratitude of every social reformer."—*Weekly Journal.*

"It is written with singular force and clearness. The author is plainly, deeply, solemnly convinced of the importance of the thing he is speaking about."—*Daily Review.*

"So enormous, so deadly, in every sense, are the evils of this pawn-system, and so frightfully on the increase, that we would be very glad to see the plan proposed in this able, earnest, and telling pamphlet fully discussed and tried. Its revelations and its facts are dreadful enough. It is like opening that door not far from the gate of the Celestial City, on the other side of the Hill, in the Pilgrim's Progress, and seeing and hearing the sweltering horrors of the damned."—*Scotsman.*

DUNVARLICH;

OR,

ROUND ABOUT THE BUSH.

In Cloth, 2s. 6d.

"An eminently readable tale, containing passages of singular power and beauty."—*Glasgow Herald.*

"Rapidity of action, vivid portraits of character in upper and lower life, sparkling wit and broad Norland humour, graphic description, in a style as clear and lively as a Highland torrent, are the main features of this new tale."—*Alloa Advertiser.*

"The author writes with ease and vigour; individualizes his characters with a few bold touches, preserving their consistency throughout; can be humorous, pathetic, or comical, as occasion requires, and indulges but sparingly in temperance lecturing."—*Perthshire Advertiser.*

"Mr. Macrae holds his own yet with any temperance novelist that has appeared."—*Daily Review.*

A LEAP-YEAR WOOING.

"This little sketch of life in lodgings will afford amusement to both sexes, and to both old and young. Bashful youths like Tom Pidger will learn from it how to 'pop the question,' and impatient maidens, availing themselves of the precious privilege of leap-year, will see how delicately and effectually the wooing from their side may be done. The revolution effected in Tom's philosophy, dress, manners, and habits, from the hour he fell in love, is amazing, but not without example in real life; and Mr. Macrae, in the few pages at his disposal, has happily hit off more than one of the vagaries of human nature."—*Morning Journal.*

"Full of rich humour and graphic description of character."—*Saturday Post.*

GEORGE HARRINGTON.

The *Scotsman* says:—"The style is keen and strong—the fun genuine; and the death of Little Tiz is, to our mind, very beautiful. We do not envy any one who could read it aloud."

The *Glasgow Herald* says:—"His narrative abounds in incidents of the most varied and interesting description. We have touches of pathos which move the heart, and humorous events and recitals which may set the table in a roar. His delineations of natural scenery are graceful, truthful, and tinted with the pencil of the poet."

The *Mercury* says:—"The interest is at times painfully intense. The author is equally successful in delineating the tender and the terrible; and with both these elements his book is replete. . . . . One chapter, describing the anxious mother waiting and watching through the long silent night for her absent son, for whom her fears have become excited, strikes us as particularly powerful, displaying a power of minute psychological anatomy which reminds us of Victor Hugo himself."

The *Court Circular* says:—"A powerfully told and most interesting story."

The *Brighton Examiner* says:—"We have rarely seen the workings of the human mind so forcibly illustrated. The events, although highly drawn, are strikingly natural; the characters are extremely well delineated; the language is simple, forcible, and appropriate, and the whole story gives terrible evidence of the dire effects of intemperance, and more especially the danger of inducing the habit of taking stimulating drinks, in the young."

The *British Standard* says:—"The book overflows with incident and with pathos. It is a most impressive and awful lesson of the bitter consequences of sin."

DIOGENES AMONG THE D.D.'s.

A BOOK OF BURLESQUES.

The *Star* says:—"These squibs were read on their first appearance with great avidity. Some of the principal—such as the 'Trial of Dr. Macleod for the Murder of Moses Law,' and the 'Courtship of Widow Freekirk'—are connected with events which must to some extent prove historical, and which it is of importance to understand; and future historians will find it of advantage to ponder the reflections of this cynic of the nineteenth century, even as we meditate and laugh over the pungent wit and rough humour of Swift, or look with mingled admiration and fear on the sharp and polished shafts of Junius."

The REV. GEORGE GILFILLAN says:—"Diogenes among the D.D.'s is one of the cleverest collections of squibs I have read for many a day. It hits these queer, quarrelling, 'tempest-in-teapot' times of ours in Scotland between 'wind and water.' The author has a keen eye for the ludicrous, and detects it, and drags it forth from under the awful wig or gray solemn semicircle surmounting even a Doctor's brows. He is not afraid to 'speak truth of dignities;' yet there is no malice in his pleasantry, no ferocity in his fun, no 'kick in his gallop.' He is more the John Leech than the Gilray of caricaturists, and seems to like those best at whom he laughs most heartily. The popularity of his 'Moses Law,' which for a time was unprecedented, has been well sustained by his others; such as his 'Trial of Dr. Norman O'Barony,' and his 'Widow Freekirk's Courtship.'"

The *Fifeshire Journal* says:—"His satire scarcely veils his deep reverence for the higher religious sentiments, and the general structure of his *jeux d'esprit* is creditable not only to his literary ability, but to his faith, which is manly in its strength, and quite refreshing in its tone. There is so much of folly now-a-days, and so little effective shooting at it as it flies, that we welcome most cordially an archer so skilful as the author of this most amusing book."

The *Greenock Telegraph* says:—"Mr. Macrae is evidently a man of large intelligence, intense convictions, and purity of motive. There is a moral earnestness visible in these amusing miscellanies which we would wish to see shared by many who will probably be foremost in censuring them. He has arrived at some conclusions which are by no means popular; especially in respect to the great politico-ecclesiastical questions of the day; yet he announces them with a candour and courage which we would wish to see more common among the leaders and guides of public opinion both in the pulpit and the press. He is not one of the great multitude which cannot be at the trouble and cost of forming an opinion on such a subject as England's attitude towards the inferior races which have been committed to her care; and, while many a solemn defender of the faith is too timid to say a word for the down-trodden and oppressed victims of a godless civilization, Mr. Macrae speaks out freely and fearlessly, making good the honest profession of his manly preface, that he has paid less respect to persons than to truth."

For List of other Works by the same Author see Advertisements.

JUST PUBLISHED, ON TONED PAPER,

ONE HUNDRED SONGS,

WITH MELODIES, ORIGINAL AND SELECTED.

By JAMES BALLANTINE,

Author of "CASTLES IN THE AIR."

SPECIMEN PAGE.

CASTLES IN THE AIR.

Music adapted by R. ADAMS.

Published with Accompaniments by David Swan, Glasgow.

Con sentimento.

The bon-nie, bon-nie bairn, sits po-kin' in the ase,

Glow'rin' in the fire wi' his wee round face;

Laughin' at the fuf-fin' lowe— what sees he there?

Ha! the young dreamer's biggin' castles in the air.

His wee chubby face, an' his touzie curly pow, Are laughin' an' noddin'

to the dancin' lowe; He'll brown his rosy cheeks, an' singe his sunny hair,

Glow'rin' at the imps wi' their castles in the air.

In Handsome Binding, Cloth Extra, Gilt Edges, Price 5s.; Post Free, 64 Stamps. In Tartan Boards, 7s. 6d.; Post Free for 94 Stamps.

GLASGOW: JOHN S. MARR & SONS.

SCOTTISH SONGS,
WITH MUSIC.

SPECIMEN PAGE:

THE FLOWERS O' THE FOREST.

Words by Mrs. Cockburn.

I've seen the smil-ing of for-tune be-guil-ing, I've tast-ed her plea-sures and felt her de-cay; Sweet was her bless-ing and kind her ca-ress-ing, But now they are fied, they are fled far a-way. I've seen the fo-rest a-dorn-ed the fore-most, Wi' flowers o' the fair-est baith pleas-ant and gay, Sae bon-nie was their blooming, their scent the air per-fum-ing, But now they are with-er'd and a' wede a-way.

I've seen the morning
With gold the hills adorning,
And loud tempests storming before the mid-day.
I've seen Tweed's silver streams,
Shining in the sunny beams,
Grow drumly and dark as he row'd on his way.

Oh! fickle fortune!
Why this cruel sporting?
Oh! why still perplex us poor sons of a day.
Thy frown canna fear me,
Thy smile canna cheer me,
Since the flowers o' the forest are a' wede away.

CONTAINING the WORDS and MUSIC of 222 POPULAR SCOTTISH SONGS, many of them Copyright. In Paper Covers, 9d.; Post Free for 10 Stamps. In Cloth Limp, 1s.; Post Free for 14 Stamps. Handsomely Bound in Cloth, Gilt, Price, 1s. 6d.; Post Free for 20 Stamps. In Tartan Boards, Price, 5s.; Post Free for 64 Stamps.

GLASGOW: JOHN S. MARR & SONS.

www.ingramcontent.com/pod-product-compliance
Lightning Source LLC
LaVergne TN
LVHW061309060426
835507LV00019B/2077